S   h

KT-514-341

Independence Educational Publishers

First published by Independence Educational Publishers

The Studio, High Green

Great Shelford

Cambridge CB22 5EG

England

© Independence 2014

Copyright

Photocopy licence

British Library Cataloguing in Publication Data

Smoking and health. -- (Issues ; 261)

1. Smoking. 2. Tobacco--Physiological effect.

I. Series II. Acred, Cara editor.

362.2'96-dc23

ISBN-13: 9781861686763

Printed in Great Britain

MWL Print Group Ltd

Contents

Chapter 1: Smoking and cigarettes

What are the health risks of smoking?	1
Tobacco	2
Smoking: a brief history	3
Why is smoking so addictive?	4
Smoking statistics	6
Effects of smoking	8
The cost of smoking	9
Paan, bidi and shisha	10
E-cigarettes – the unanswered questions	11
Watch out, e-cigarette smokers – you're inhaling the unknown	13
Passive smoking	14
E-cigarettes 'could encourage young people to take up smoking', says research	14
New film ignites the dangers of third-hand smoke	15
Brits unaware of signs of lung cancer	16
Health check: how harmful is social smoking?	17
The impact of smoking in films on young people	18
More than 200,000 UK children start smoking every year	20

Chapter 2: Quitting and trends

Quitting is the best thing you'll ever do	21
Doctors back denial of treatment for smokers and the obese	22
Stop smoking services help 20,000 quit	24
Smoke and mirrors	25
Stoptober challenge reaches new high as country's biggest mass quit attempt	26
Public Health Committee MEPs toughen up plans to deter young people from smoking	27
MPs vote in favour of banning smoking in cars with child passengers despite opposition	28
The last bastion: smoking to be banned in prisons	29
New York bans tobacco sales to under-21s	30
European smoking bans: evolution of the legislation	31
Fewer premature births due to smoking ban	32
'Tobacco marketing harmful to kids'	33
Thumbs down for Tobacco Products Directive	34
TMA responds to the Government's decision not to introduce plain packaging	35
Scotland aims to be smoke-free by 2034 but what about e-cigs?	36
Indonesia's tobacco children	38

Key facts	40
Glossary	41
Assignments	42
Index	43
Acknowledgements	44

Introduction

Smoking and Health is Volume 261 in the ***ISSUES*** series. The aim of the series is to offer current, diverse information about important issues in our world, from a UK perspective.

ABOUT SMOKING AND HEALTH

The news that smoking cigarettes is detrimental to your health is not a recent revelation, yet every year 100,000 people die from smoking and even more from smoking-related illnesses. This book examines the effects that smoking has on the body, the reasons behind its addictive nature and the dangers of passive and social smoking. It also considers the recent trend towards e-cigarettes, asking whether they are an effective tool to aid quitting or a device we don't yet know enough about.

OUR SOURCES

Titles in the ***ISSUES*** series are designed to function as educational resource books, providing a balanced overview of a specific subject.

The information in our books is comprised of facts, articles and opinions from many different sources, including:

⇨ Newspaper reports and opinion pieces

⇨ Website factsheets

⇨ Magazine and journal articles

⇨ Statistics and surveys

⇨ Government reports

⇨ Literature from special interest groups

A NOTE ON CRITICAL EVALUATION

Because the information reprinted here is from a number of different sources, readers should bear in mind the origin of the text and whether the source is likely to have a particular bias when presenting information (or when conducting their research). It is hoped that, as you read about the many aspects of the issues explored in this book, you will critically evaluate the information presented.

It is important that you decide whether you are being presented with facts or opinions. Does the writer give a biased or unbiased report? If an opinion is being expressed, do you agree with the writer? Is there potential bias to the 'facts' or statistics behind an article?

ASSIGNMENTS

In the back of this book, you will find a selection of assignments designed to help you engage with the articles you have been reading and to explore your own opinions. Some tasks will take longer than others and there is a mixture of design, writing and research-based activities that you can complete alone or in a group.

FURTHER RESEARCH

At the end of each article we have listed its source and a website that you can visit if you would like to conduct your own research. Please remember to critically evaluate any sources that you consult and consider whether the information you are viewing is accurate and unbiased.

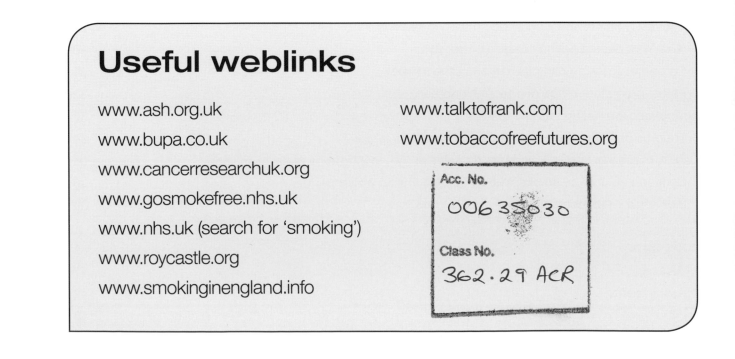

Useful weblinks

www.ash.org.uk

www.bupa.co.uk

www.cancerresearchuk.org

www.gosmokefree.nhs.uk

www.nhs.uk (search for 'smoking')

www.roycastle.org

www.smokinginengland.info

www.talktofrank.com

www.tobaccofreefutures.org

What are the health risks of smoking?

Smoking is one of the biggest causes of death and illness in the UK.

Every year, around 100,000 people die from smoking, with many more deaths caused by smoking-related illnesses.

Smoking increases your risk of developing more than 50 serious health conditions. Some may be fatal and others can cause irreversible long-term damage to your health.

You can become ill:

⇨ if you smoke yourself

⇨ through other people's smoke (passive smoking or secondhand smoke).

Health risks

Smoking causes about 90% of lung cancers. It also causes cancer in many other parts of the body including the:

⇨ mouth

⇨ lips

⇨ throat

⇨ voice box (larynx)

⇨ oesophagus (the tube between your mouth and stomach)

⇨ bladder

⇨ kidney

⇨ liver

⇨ stomach

⇨ pancreas.

Smoking damages your heart and your blood circulation, increasing your risk of developing conditions such as:

⇨ coronary heart disease

⇨ heart attack

⇨ stroke

⇨ peripheral vascular disease (damaged blood vessels)

⇨ cerebrovascular disease (damaged arteries that supply blood to your brain).

Smoking also damages your lungs, leading to conditions such as:

⇨ chronic bronchitis (infection of the main airways in the lungs)

⇨ emphysema (damage to the small airways in the lungs)

⇨ pneumonia (inflammation in the lungs).

Smoking can also worsen or prolong the symptoms of respiratory conditions, such as asthma, or respiratory tract infections, such as the common cold.

In men, smoking can cause impotence because it limits the blood supply to the penis. It can also affect the fertility of both men and women, making it difficult for you to have children.

Secondhand smoke

Secondhand smoke comes from the tip of a lit cigarette and the smoke that the smoker breathes out.

People who breathe in secondhand smoke are at risk of getting the same health conditions as smokers, particularly lung cancer and heart disease. For example, breathing in secondhand smoke increases a non-smoker's risk of developing lung cancer or heart disease by about 25%.

Babies and children are particularly vulnerable to the effects of secondhand smoke. A child who is exposed to smoke is at increased risk of developing respiratory infections, a chronic cough and, if they have asthma, their symptoms will get worse. They're also at increased risk of sudden infant death syndrome (SIDS) and glue ear.

Smoking during pregnancy

If you smoke when you're pregnant, you put your unborn baby's health at risk, as well as your own. Smoking during pregnancy increases the risk of complications, such as:

⇨ miscarriage

⇨ premature (early) birth

⇨ a low birth weight baby

⇨ stillbirth

Getting help

Your GP will be able to give you information and advice about quitting smoking. You can also call:

⇨ the NHS Smokefree helpline on 0300 123 1044

⇨ the NHS Pregnancy Smoking Helpline on 0800 169 9 169

28 November 2013

⇨ The above information is reprinted with kind permission from NHS Choices. Please visit www.nhs.uk for further information.

Tobacco

What is tobacco?

Tobacco is found in cigarettes which you smoke. It comes from the leaves of the tobacco plant and contains many different chemicals.

One of the chemicals is nicotine, which gives smokers their 'hit' but is also highly addictive. This means it can be hard to quit smoking even if you want to.

Regular smokers believe that smoking tobacco helps them to relax, to handle stress and to feel less hungry.

But smoking can make your clothes and breath smell and can affect your skin and hair.

It can also cause serious damage to your health – it's a risk factor for emphysema, heart attacks, strokes and lung cancer. It's estimated that smoking tobacco contributes to 100,000 premature deaths in the UK every year.

Appearance

The green leaves of the tobacco plant are picked, dried and then rubbed to produce a brown, flaky mixture.

It can then be bought loose as rolling tobacco which you use to create hand-rolled cigarettes or in ready-made cigarettes.

It doesn't matter how you smoke tobacco, all forms have risks.

There are many different brands of cigarettes and most come in packs of ten, 14 or 20.

The financial cost of being a smoker depends on the scale of their habit, but as a rough guide, smoking 20 a day for one year will cost over £2,700.

Use

Tobacco is most often smoked as a cigarette or in a pipe, but tobacco is available in a chewable form and in a form, called snuff, that can be sniffed.

Shisha is the smoking of fruit flavoured tobacco using a water pipe. The tobacco is burnt and the smoke is sucked through the water pipe, which cools the smoke down allowing it to be breathed in by the smoker. However, smoking Shisha for one hour can deliver the same health risks as smoking 100 cigarettes

Shisha is a part of Middle Eastern and Indian culture, but it seems to be becoming increasingly popular in the UK among non-Middle Eastern and Indian groups.

The effects

Regular smokers believe that smoking tobacco helps them to relax, to handle stress and to feel less hungry.

However, tobacco smoke (tar) contains over 4,000 chemicals and many have effects on various parts of the human body, including the brain, lungs, heart and mouth.

Most of the cancers associated with smoking are due to the tar in the smoke.

Smoking any drug gets it to the brain very quickly. When a tobacco smoker inhales it's estimated that the nicotine in the tobacco smoke reaches the brain in around eight seconds.

This speed of action contributes to a user becoming hooked to the nicotine in tobacco.

What are the risks of tobacco?

First-time smokers often feel sick and dizzy.

Smoking tobacco has lots of immediate effects such as making your clothes and hair smell, to costing you lots of money. Smoking stops oxygen getting to the skin making you more prone to spots and a dull complexion. Over time it can lead to premature aging, meaning more wrinkles and a so-called 'cats bum' mouth. Smoking can also make hair less shiny and yellow nails and teeth.

Of the over 4,000 chemicals that tobacco contains many have harsh effects on the human body. Smoking can increase your blood pressure and the heart rate, which can damage the heart and circulation and contribute to heart attacks, strokes and cause cancer. Also:

⇨ Smokers are more likely to get coughs and chest infections.

⇨ Long-term use could leave you with cancer, emphysema or heart disease.

⇨ Smoking when pregnant can harm the foetus and can even cause a miscarriage.

⇨ It's not uncommon for babies born to mothers who have smoked during pregnancy to have a lower than normal birth weight, which, some have linked to autism and sudden infant death syndrome.

⇨ Smoking has been linked to the amputation of 2,000 limbs a year.

⇨ It's estimated smoking contributes to 100,000 premature deaths in the UK every year.

⇨ Other people breathing in your smoke could end up with breathing difficulties, asthma or even cancer.

⇨ Smoking shisha can be more dangerous than smoking a cigarettes, with users at increased risk of picking up diseases such as herpes or tuberculosis from sharing pipes.

Impurities

'Black market' cigarettes and rolling tobacco are either counterfeit or brought into the UK from other countries. There is no way of knowing what is in a counterfeit cigarette or rolling tobacco and what effect it could have on you.

Even if tobacco has not been bought on the black market, the smoke contains over 4,000 chemicals and many of them are known to do nasty things to the human body including causing cancer.

Some of the ingredients contained in cigarettes are listed below:

⇨ Ammonia: A common ingredient found in household cleaners and also contained in urine

⇨ Arsenic: A deadly poison used to kill rats

⇨ Butane: Gas that is used in lighter fluid

⇨ Carbon monoxide: A poisonous gas that is contained in car fumes

⇨ Cadmium: Used in batteries

⇨ Methanol: Rocket fuel

⇨ Acetone: Used in paint thinner and nail varnish remover

⇨ Formaldehyde: Used for embalming dead bodies

⇨ Acrolein: Formerly used as a chemical weapon

⇨ Tar: A material used to make roads

⇨ Hydrogen cyanide: The poison that was used in gas chambers.

Can you get addicted to tobacco?

Yes. Tobacco contains nicotine, a highly addictive drug. Smokers can get hooked very quickly and it can take years and a huge effort to kick the habit. Many people who smoke wish they had not started in the first place.

Not many people are able to remain occasional smokers because nicotine is a very addictive substance.

For friendly and practical advice on giving up smoking call the NHS Smoking Helpline on 0800 169 0 169.

The law

It's illegal for shopkeepers to sell tobacco or tobacco products to anyone under 18.

Cigarettes must be sold in their original packaging and it is illegal to sell single cigarettes to anyone, adult or child.

⇨ The above information is reprinted with kind permission from Talk to Frank. Please visit www.talktofrank.com for further information.

© Crown copyright 2014

Smoking: a brief history

1000 BC

The first recorded instances of smoking. The Mayan civilisation smoked the leaves of the tobacco plant.

1492

Christopher Columbus was probably the first European to see the tobacco plant – but he did not smoke!

1560

A French ambassador, Jean Nicot, sent tobacco and seeds from Brazil to Paris, saying they had health benefits. The tobacco plant is named *Nicotiana tabacum* after Nicot, as is nicotine.

1604

King James I introduced a tax on tobacco. A staunch anti-smoker, he wrote *A Counterblaste to Tobacco*, which told of his dislike for tobacco and smoking!

1761

Snuff users were warned of the dangers of developing nasal cancer.

1868

Smoke-free railway carriages were introduced.

1908

The sale of tobacco to under-16s was banned.

1956

It was proven that tobacco smoking increased the risk of lung cancer and other diseases.

1984

The first No Smoking Day in the UK was held.

1992

Smoking could be listed as a cause of death on death certificates.

1999

Tobacco advertising was banned in the UK.

2006

Scotland became smoke free (in enclosed public spaces). England, Wales and Northern Ireland followed suit in 2007.

⇨ The above information is reprinted with kind permission from White Ribbon. Please visit www.white-ribbon.org.uk for further information.

© White Ribbon 2014

Why is smoking so addictive?

If two-thirds of all smokers want to stop smoking, and every year nearly three in ten smokers try to do so, why are there not more ex-smokers than smokers? What is it that makes cigarettes so addictive and makes quitting smoking so challenging?

It's not just the nicotine that makes smoking addictive – it's a mixture of behavioural habits, social and environmental influences, and maybe even your genes. This article will explain more about these causes and how you can overcome them to successfully stop smoking.

What is nicotine?

Cigarettes contain the drug nicotine. Nicotine creates a complex form of addiction, which makes you want to smoke, even if you would prefer to stop. Every time you smoke a cigarette, it creates and reinforces this addiction. If you stop smoking, you get nicotine withdrawal symptoms.

Nicotine is an addictive drug, meaning you can become physically and psychologically dependent on it. This means you get withdrawal symptoms if you don't smoke. When you smoke, nicotine is absorbed through the lining of your lungs into your blood and this distributes it around your body. It can also enter your blood in other ways,

such as through your nose if you use snuff. Nicotine replacement therapy (NRT) patches and gum make use of its ability to be absorbed through your skin or mouth.

Effects on your heart and blood vessels

Nicotine increases your heart rate and blood pressure. However, over time, you can become tolerant to this effect. This means that if you use nicotine regularly, over time, your heart will begin to respond less to it.

Effects on your brain and mood

After inhaling, it takes seven to ten seconds for nicotine to reach your brain. It's both a stimulant and a depressant drug, which means that it can give you a boost but can also bring on a feeling of relaxation. It's partly these powerful effects that make it so addictive.

Nicotine can make you feel dizzy, nervous or give you a headache. However, nicotine also temporarily reduces stress and can make you feel more content. This is because it causes a chemical called dopamine to be released – dopamine is associated with feelings of pleasure. This also contributes to making nicotine highly addictive because after a while, nicotine reduces your brain's ability to get these same feelings. Therefore,

you need more nicotine, and hence more cigarettes, to get the same effect.

Over time, as you get more addicted, your body gets used to functioning with the effects of nicotine. Between cigarettes you get withdrawal symptoms, which can include:

⇨ cravings for nicotine

⇨ feeling angry or irritable

⇨ having trouble concentrating

⇨ headaches

⇨ feeling tired

⇨ digestive problems (such as constipation)

⇨ an increased appetite and weight gain.

These feelings can make you reach for another cigarette – although it may seem that smoking prevents these, what it's really doing is just briefly relieving your withdrawal symptoms. When you stop smoking, withdrawal symptoms can make it very tempting to start again, and this is why it can be so difficult to quit.

Understanding why you smoke

Although nicotine is to blame for making smoking addictive, your

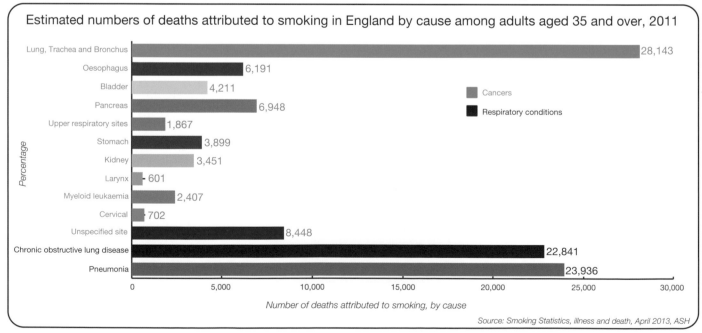

Estimated numbers of deaths attributed to smoking in England by cause among adults aged 35 and over, 2011

- Lung, Trachea and Bronchus: 28,143
- Oesophagus: 6,191
- Bladder: 4,211
- Pancreas: 6,948
- Upper respiratory sites: 1,867
- Stomach: 3,899
- Kidney: 3,451
- Larynx: 601
- Myeloid leukaemia: 2,407
- Cervical: 702
- Unspecified site: 8,448
- Chronic obstructive lung disease: 22,841
- Pneumonia: 23,936

Cancers
Respiratory conditions

Percentage

Number of deaths attributed to smoking, by cause

Source: Smoking Statistics, illness and death, April 2013, ASH

reliance on cigarettes may well be strengthened by emotional and psychological factors. These are different for everyone so if you understand the reasons why you smoke, it should make it easier to stop.

You may have started smoking when you were young, perhaps because it was fashionable or rebellious, or because your parents or friends smoked. However, it's likely that over time your relationship with smoking has changed. Maybe now you're more likely to have a cigarette to break up the day, when you're out with friends who also smoke or because you're having an alcoholic drink.

A great way to understand your reasons for smoking is to keep a diary for a week. Every time you smoke, write down:

⇨ the time

⇨ the place

⇨ what you're doing

⇨ who you're with

⇨ how you feel before having the cigarette

⇨ how you feel after having the cigarette.

After a week, you should be able to see trends and patterns to your smoking, which may help to reveal habits and reasons for smoking that you weren't aware of before.

Common reasons for smoking

'Smoking makes me feel good'

Cigarettes contain nicotine, which is not only addictive but also a powerful stimulant. After inhaling cigarette smoke, it takes just seconds for the nicotine to enter your blood and reach your brain. Once there, it stimulates the release of chemicals. This gives you an instant rush, making you feel more alert and speeding up your reaction time. However, as with any addictive behaviour, for every high there is a low – as the effects of the nicotine start to wear off, the withdrawal symptoms start, and so you reach for the next cigarette.

'Smoking helps me to relax when I'm stressed'

You probably find that cigarettes help to calm you down when you feel stressed. In reality, researchers can't be sure whether nicotine really helps to reduce anxiety and makes you more relaxed. It's likely that it's just relieving feelings of withdrawal symptoms that come on within hours or even minutes of your last cigarette. These can make you feel grumpy or agitated, and you're likely to have trouble concentrating. Feeding your nicotine addiction reverses these effects and makes you feel calmer, and so because of this, you begin to associate smoking with feeling relaxed.

'Smoking helps me to socialise'

It's possible that cigarettes provide you with a way to start friendships and make socialising easier through a shared common interest. You may ask someone for a match or lighter to help start a conversation, or use your smoking habit to bond with work colleagues – after all, cigarettes give you an excuse to have a break and a chance to catch up on office gossip. But stopping smoking needn't mean an end to this – going for a coffee or doing a crossword together can be great alternatives.

'Smoking gives me something to do'

Maybe you use cigarettes as a distraction in difficult situations, particularly because it gives you something to do with your hands. Or perhaps you smoke to help break up the monotony of doing a tedious job or writing a long essay. But there are plenty of other ways to relieve boredom and anxiety. Why not invest in a stress ball or thinking putty, or if you need a break from a boring task, make a cup of tea or go for a walk around the block.

Action points

Break the cycle of nicotine addiction by reminding yourself that every time you smoke, you're only getting rid of the withdrawal symptoms in the short term.

Keep a smoking diary to help you understand why you smoke.

Find other ways to relax when you're stressed, such as breathing exercises or phoning a friend for a chat.

Don't smoke just for something to do – find something else to occupy your hands and mind.

October 2012

⇨ The above information is reprinted with kind permission from Bupa. Please visit www.bupa.co.uk for further information.

I took up smoking to make friends...

Smoking statistics

Who smokes and how much.

Smoking trends in Great Britain

The highest recorded level of smoking among men in Great Britain was 82% in 1948, of which 65% smoked manufactured cigarettes. At that time, significant numbers of men smoked pipes or cigars as well as, or instead of, manufactured cigarettes. By contrast, women have tended to smoke only cigarettes. Smoking prevalence among women in 1948 was 41% and remained fairly constant until the early 1970s, peaking at 45% in the mid 1960s.[1]

Overall prevalence among adults (aged 16 and over) has been declining since questions about smoking were first included in the annual lifestyle survey. The biggest fall was between 1974 and 1994. Since then the proportion of adults smoking continued to decline but at a slower rate. However, since 2007 the rate of smoking has remained largely unchanged.[2]

There are about ten million adult cigarette smokers in Great Britain and about 15 million ex-smokers.[3] Since 1990 there has been a steady increase in the number of smokers using mainly hand-rolled tobacco. In 1990, 18% of male smokers and 2% of female smokers said they smoked mainly hand-rolled cigarettes but by 2011 this had risen to 40% and 26%, respectively.[4] In 2012, the OPN survey found that 38% of men and 24% of women smoked hand-rolled cigarettes.[2]

Measuring smoking rates

Periodically the Government sets targets to reduce smoking prevalence in the population. In the 1998 White Paper 'Smoking kills', the Government set a target to reduce adult smoking rates to 21% or less by 2010, with a reduction in prevalence among routine and manual groups to 26% or less.[5] The latest national survey shows that the target for the general population has been achieved but not that for lower socio-economic groups (33% in 2012).

In its strategy paper launched on 1 February 2010, the Labour Government set new targets to reduce smoking among the general population to 10% of adults and to 1% or less among children by 2020.[6] In March 2011, the Coalition Government launched its Tobacco Control Plan for England in which it set out ambitions to reduce adult smoking prevalence to 18.5% or less by 2015 and to reduce smoking among 15-year-olds to 12% or less by 2015.[7]

Cigarette smoking and age

Smoking continues to be lowest among people aged 60 and over. Although they are more likely than younger people to have ever been smokers, they are more likely to have stopped smoking. While smoking prevalence among young adults aged 16–19 appears to be declining more rapidly than in other age groups, it is possible that this may be due to a degree of under-reporting by young people.[2]

Number of secondary school children in England who smoke

Very few children are smokers when they start secondary school: among 11-year-olds fewer than 0.5% are regular smokers. The likelihood of smoking increases with age so that by 15 years of age 10% of pupils are regular smokers.[8]

Overall, the prevalence of regular smoking among children aged 11-15 remained stable at between nine and 11% from 1998 until 2006. However, in 2007 there was a fall in overall prevalence from 9% to 6%, the lowest rate recorded since surveys of pupils' smoking began in 1982. The downward trend has continued: in 2012, overall prevalence was 4% and among 15-year-olds it fell to 10%.[8]

Cigarette smoking and socio-economic group

There is a strong link between cigarette smoking and socio-economic group. In 2012, 33% of men and 32% of women in routine

Cigarette smoking by age – % of adult population

	Age					
	16-19	20-24	25-34	35-49	50-59	60+
1978	34	44	45	45	45	30
1988	26	37	36	36	33	23
1998	31	40	35	31	28	16
2008	22	30	27	24	22	13
2009	24	26	25	25	21	14
2010	19	27	26	24	20	13
2011	18	29	23	24	19	13
2012	15	29	27	23	21	13

Source: Smoking statistics, October 2013, ASH.

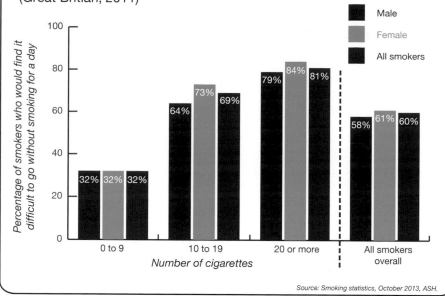

Proportion of smokers who would find it difficult to go without smoking for a day by sex and number of cigarettes smoked per day (Great Britian, 2011)

Percentage of smokers who would find it difficult to go without smoking for a day

Male
Female
All smokers

0 to 9: 32% 32% 32%
10 to 19: 64% 73% 69%
20 or more: 79% 84% 81%
All smokers overall: 58% 61% 60%

Number of cigarettes

Source: Smoking statistics, October 2013, ASH.

and manual occupations smoked compared to 16% of men and 12% of women in managerial and professional occupations.[2]

Historically there has been a slower decline in smoking among manual groups, resulting in smoking becoming increasingly concentrated in this population. In recent years, smoking rates have fallen by a similar amount across all social groups, so that the differential between non-manual and manual has not changed significantly.

Previous ONS surveys have revealed an association between socio-economic group and the age at which people started to smoke. The 2011 GLF survey revealed that in managerial and professional households, 31% had started smoking before they were 16, compared with 45% of those in routine and manual households.

Trends in cigarette consumption

Consumption of manufactured cigarettes among adult male smokers rose from 14 per day in 1948 to 19 per day in 1955, and remained at about this level until 1970 when there was an increase to 22 per day by 1973. Among female smokers, consumption rose steadily from seven cigarettes per

day in 1949 to a maximum of 17 per day in 1976.[1]

Since the mid-1970s, cigarette consumption has fallen among both men and women with average reported consumption now at 12 cigarettes per smoker per day.[2] As in previous years, men smoked slightly more per day on average than women and there was an association between consumption and socio-economic group, although the difference between groups is now small. In 2012, smokers in manual occupations smoked an average of 12 cigarettes a day compared with ten a day for those in managerial or professional groups.

Dependence on cigarette smoking

In 2011, 63% of smokers said they would like to stop smoking altogether. Other ways of measuring dependence include how difficult people would find it to go for a whole day without smoking and how soon they smoke after waking.[4]

First cigarette of the day

In 2011, 16% of all smokers had their first cigarette within five minutes of waking. Among smokers of 20 or more cigarettes a day, 35% smoked their first cigarette of the day within five minutes of waking, compared to just 3% of those smoking fewer than ten a day.[4]

Managing without a cigarette for the whole day

In 2011, 60% of smokers said they would find it hard to go for a whole day without smoking. 81% of heavier smokers (20 or more a day) said they would find it difficult, compared to 32% of those smoking fewer than ten cigarettes per day.[4]

References

1. Wald, N. and Nicolaides-Bouman, A. *UK Smoking Statistics. 2nd edition*, Oxford University Press, 1991

2. *Opinions and Lifestyle Survey, Smoking habits amongst adults, 2012.* ONS, Sept. 2013

3. Calculation derived from ONS Population Estimates, mid-2012 (England & Wales), General Register Office for Scotland, 2012. Opinions and Lifestyle Survey, Smoking habits amongst adults, 2012. ONS, Sept. 2013

4. *2011 General Lifestyle Survey.* Office for National Statistics, March 2013

5. *PSA Delivery Agreement 18: Promote better health and well-being for all.* The Treasury, Oct 2007 (PDF)

6. *A Smokefree Future. A comprehensive tobacco control strategy for England.* Department of Health, 2010.

7. *Healthy Lives, Healthy People: A Tobacco Control Plan for England.* HM Government, March 2011

8. *Smoking drinking and drug use among young people in England in 2012.* The Information Centre for Health and Social Care, 2013.

October 2013

⇨ The above information is reprinted with kind permission from Action on Smoking and Health (ASH). Please visit www.ash.org.uk for further information.

Effects of smoking

Smoking causes serious health problems, many of them life-threatening. In the UK more than 100,000 people die each year from smoking-related diseases – this means about half of all regular smokers will die because of their addiction.

This article will focus on the harm smoking does to your body and the diseases it causes.

Smoking and cancer

Smoking is by far the greatest avoidable risk for developing many types of cancer including throat, mouth, oesophagus, lung, stomach, kidney, bladder and cervical (neck of the womb). It's also linked to some types of leukaemia (cancer of the white blood cells).

Key facts

⇨ About nine out of ten lung cancers are caused by smoking, either directly or through passive smoking.

⇨ If you smoke, you're approximately three times more likely to develop bladder cancer than someone who has never smoked.

⇨ Hand-rolled cigarettes have a greater effect than manufactured ones on your risk of developing mouth cancer.

Smoking and your heart and circulation

Smoking damages your blood vessels and increases your risk of heart disease and stroke. It can also affect how well your blood, and therefore oxygen, flows around your body – for example, you may notice you often have cold hands and feet, which is a result of not enough blood getting to them.

Key facts

⇨ If you smoke 20 or more cigarettes a day, your risk of having a stroke can be up to six times that of a non-smoker.

⇨ If you're under 40 and a smoker, you're five times more likely to have a heart attack than a non-smoker of the same age.

⇨ Smoking makes you up to 16 times more likely to develop blocked blood vessels in your legs or feet. This can lead to gangrene (where tissues in your body die) and possibly the need for amputation.

⇨ The risk of developing a blood clot (deep vein thrombosis, DVT) is greater if you smoke. If you're a woman who smokes and you're taking the contraceptive pill, you're nearly nine times more likely to develop DVT than a woman who doesn't smoke and doesn't take the contraceptive pill.

Smoking and your lungs

It's hardly surprising that if you're regularly breathing in smoke, your airways can become damaged, making it harder for you to get air in and out of your lungs. When your lungs are damaged in this way, it's called chronic obstructive pulmonary disease (COPD). COPD describes a number of long-term lung conditions that cause breathing difficulties, the main two of which are bronchitis and emphysema. Smoking can also mean that if you get flu, you're more likely to develop complications.

Key facts

⇨ Nearly nine out of ten people who die from COPD are smokers.

⇨ If you smoke, you're more likely to get pneumonia – the more you smoke, and the longer you have smoked, the greater your risk.

⇨ Children of parents who smoke are more likely to have asthma or other breathing problems.

Smoking and sex

It might be news to you but smoking can seriously affect your sex life and both men's and women's fertility. It can also harm your unborn child during pregnancy and after he or she is born.

Key facts

⇨ Smoking not only makes men more likely to have erectile dysfunction, but it also damages sperm and reduces how much of it is produced.

⇨ If you smoke and are taking the contraceptive pill, you're 20 times more likely to have a heart attack than a woman who doesn't smoke.

⇨ On average, women who smoke go through the menopause two years earlier than women who don't smoke.

⇨ Smoking reduces fertility in both men and women, meaning it's likely to take longer for you to conceive.

⇨ If you're having fertility treatment such as in vitro fertilisation (IVF), smoking can affect how successful this is.

Smoking and your appearance

It's a harsh truth, but one of the most noticeable effects of smoking is how it affects your appearance. It also reduces your sense of taste and smell, and that smoky odour that clings to your hair and clothes isn't very attractive either.

Key facts

⇨ Smoking can prematurely age your skin by between ten and 20 years, and you're more likely to have facial wrinkles at a younger age.

- The tar in cigarettes stains your fingers and teeth, so they become discoloured and yellow.

- If you smoke, you're more likely to store fat around your waist rather than around your hips. Having this body shape, in which you have a high waist-to-hip ratio, is linked to a higher risk of developing type 2 diabetes, high blood pressure and heart disease.

- If you smoke, you're two to three times more likely to develop psoriasis than a non-smoker. Psoriasis is a skin condition that causes patches of inflamed skin.

Smoking and surgery

If you smoke and you need an operation – whether it's related to smoking or not – your body will take longer to repair itself afterwards, and you may be more at risk of complications, such as DVT, both during and after the surgery. This means a longer recovery period with more time in hospital and off work.

What if I stop smoking?

The good news is that it's never too late to stop smoking, and when you do, the risks to your health drop dramatically. Within a month of quitting, your appearance will improve. After one year, your risk of heart attack is cut in half compared with that of a smoker. And if you stay a non-smoker for ten years, you will also reduce your risk of lung cancer by half compared with someone who smokes.

Produced by Polly Kerr, Bupa Health Information Team, October 2012

- The above information is reprinted with kind permission from Bupa. Please visit www.bupa.co.uk for further information.

The cost of smoking

Smoking is an expensive habit for both your pocket and the environment. Take a look...

Your money

If you smoke the amount of cigarettes below then you are shelling out:

- five cigarettes a day for one year = £644

- ten cigarettes a day for one year = £1289

- 20 cigarettes a day for one year = £2,577.

Think of all that extra money you could be using for holidays, clothes, gadgets and football season tickets!

And scarily enough, if you smoked 40 cigarettes a day for ten years you would have spent £67,748, so instead of burning this money you could have almost bought your own flat.

These calculations were based on a pack of 20 cigarettes costing between £5.50 and £6. To find out more, use the online Cost Calculator to see what this means for you or your family.

The cost to the environment

Deforestation

Producing tobacco involves cutting down lots of trees. Forests are cleared to grow tobacco but the biggest problem is the number of trees that are cut down for fuel to dry tobacco. Tobacco is cured (dried) by heating the tobacco through burning wood. Nearly nine million acres of forests are cut down each year for fuel for curing.

Pollution and wildlife

- Tobacco farmers need to use lots of fertiliser and pesticides to protect the tobacco as it grows. With food crops, the use of chemicals is strictly monitored. Tobacco isn't a food crop so this means it isn't controlled as much and the chemicals can get into the local water supply.

- 2,700 tonnes of cigarette litter is dropped in London alone each year. Some people think that cigarette filters are biodegradable (able to decompose/break up naturally. Cigarette filters are made of a form of plastic that takes more than ten years to biodegrade.

- Cigarette butts have been found in the stomachs of fish, birds, whales and other sea creatures, who mistake them for food.

Labour

Around 86% of the world's tobacco is grown in the developing world. Producing tobacco can be expensive so tobacco farmers use child labour to cut costs. Children working on tobacco plantations often miss school and have to carry out the same work an adult does.

Tobacco harvesters can be affected by Green Tobacco sickness. People who harvest tobacco leaves absorb the nicotine through their skin, causing a variety of symptoms, including vomiting, dizziness, headaches and difficulty breathing.

2 November 2012

- The above information is reprinted with kind permission from Young Scot. Please visit www.youngscot.org for further information.

Paan, bidi and shisha

Tobacco that you don't smoke (including paan, betel quid and chewing tobacco) is not a 'safe' way to use tobacco. It causes cancer and can be as addictive as smoking. Find out the risks and how you can quit.

Chewing tobacco

Betel quid, paan or gutkha is a mixture of ingredients including betel nut (also called areca nut), herbs, spices and often tobacco, wrapped in a betel leaf. Chewing smokeless tobacco, such as paan or gutkha, is popular with many people from south Asian communities, but all forms of tobacco can harm your health. Research has shown that using smokeless tobacco raises the risk of mouth cancer and oesophageal (food pipe) cancer.

Studies have also found that betel itself can raise the risk of cancer, so chewing betel quid without tobacco is still harmful.

Cigarettes, bidi and shisha

Smoking rates are higher among Bangladeshi men (40%) and Pakistani men (29%) than in the general population (21%). Indian men and south Asian women are less likely to smoke.

Smoking increases your risk of cancer, heart disease and respiratory (breathing) disease. This is true whether you smoke bidi (thin cigarettes of tobacco wrapped in brown tendu leaf), cigarettes or shisha (also known as a water pipe or hookah).

A World Health Organization study has suggested that during one session on a hookah (around 20 to 80 minutes) a person can inhale the same amount of smoke as a cigarette smoker consuming 100 or more cigarettes. Hookah smoke also contains nicotine, cancer-causing chemicals and toxic gases such as carbon monoxide.

Quit smoking and tobacco

People who use NHS support are up to four times more likely to quit smoking than those who try to stop alone. All areas have a free local NHS Stop Smoking Service that provides medication and support to help you quit. Many services also offer support to help you stop using smokeless tobacco, such as paan.

Nine out of ten people using a stop-smoking service would recommend it to another person who wants to stop smoking. It is proven to offer you your best chance of stopping. To find your local service, go to the Smokefree website (www.nhs.uk/smokefree), or ask your doctor or nurse to refer you to your local service.

You can also call the NHS Smokefree Helpline number on 0300 123 1044 (0300 123 1014 minicom), and ask to speak to an interpreter for the language you need. The helpline is open from 9am–8pm Monday to Friday and from 11am–4pm on Saturday and Sunday.

20 January 2014

⇨ The above information is reprinted with kind permission from NHS Choices. Please visit www.nhs.uk for further information.

E-cigarettes – the unanswered questions

Five years ago you'd probably never heard of electronic cigarettes, or e-cigarettes. Now it seems you can't open a newspaper – or go into a newsagent, supermarket or pharmacist – without seeing them advertised or on sale.

For smokers concerned about the toxic cocktail of cancer-causing substances in tobacco smoke, e-cigarettes – sometimes touted as a safer alternative to smoking – might initially sound like a Holy Grail. We're determined to reduce the number of smoking-related cancers. If e-cigarettes can help reduce this toll, it's crucial to public health that this avenue is properly explored to fully understand the benefits and risks of these devices.

There are widely differing responses to the replication of the act of smoking offered by e-cigarettes use, known as vaping. Some people see a unique opportunity to promote a mass switch to vaping that would avoid the massive health toll of smoking tobacco on the one in five adults smoking in the UK today. Others see e-cigarettes as posing a great risk that would keep people too close to their cigarette habit, making a lapse back to smoking more likely.

Currently e-cigarettes are not regulated in the way that approved nicotine replacement therapies (NRT) such as patches and gum are. This means they haven't undergone all the rigorous tests needed to ensure their safety and effectiveness.

We want to see 'light touch' regulation brought in, to ensure the product's contents and delivery is monitored and consistent, they are not sold to under-18's and that their marketing does not promote smoking itself.

The increasing popularity of e-cigarettes makes it crucial to answer questions about their impact – not just on the health of smokers who use them, but on non-smokers, ex-smokers, children and society as a whole.

That's why we commissioned researchers at the University of Stirling to identify the unanswered questions and concerns around e-cigarettes, and look at the broader issue of tobacco 'harm reduction' – measures to reduce illness and death caused by tobacco use.

We've just published their report, and a summary has been published in the journal *Tobacco Control*). In this article, we'll look in more detail at the questions and issues it raises.

What are e-cigarettes?

E-cigarettes look like real cigarettes and usually consist of a battery, a cartridge containing nicotine (the addictive ingredient in tobacco), a solution of propylene glycol or glycerine mixed with water, and an atomiser (a device that turns the nicotine solution into a fine mist or vapour).

When someone inhales on the e-cigarette the nicotine solution is heated and evaporates. Research shows the e-cigarette user inhales a 'hit' of nicotine as they would when inhaling smoke from a cigarette (although other research has questioned how effective some e-cigarettes are at nicotine delivery).

Cartridges are available in different concentrations of nicotine, and in various flavours such as apple, chocolate, coffee and mint. Most e-cigarettes have an LED at the tip which lights up when someone inhales, in a similar way to the lit tip of a cigarette.

Are they really 'safer than cigarettes'?

While it's the highly addictive nicotine that keeps smokers hooked, it's the toxic cocktail of chemicals in tobacco smoke that kills half of all long-term users. Traditional tobacco cigarettes contain around 4,000 different chemicals, including toxins like arsenic and radioactive polonium-210. Tobacco smoke has long been recognised as a carcinogen responsible for more than one in four UK cancer deaths, and the biggest single cause of cancer in the world.

The lack of tobacco in e-cigarettes means they are almost certainly much safer way of getting a nicotine hit than smoking cigarettes.

But there are still some questions about the safety of the chemicals that are in e-cigarettes, and the current lack of regulation means there's no way of verifying what's actually in them, especially with so many different companies now entering the market.

For example, we know little about the safety of the propylene glycol in many e-cigarettes. And nicotine itself can be toxic in very high doses. So there are questions about the safety of leakage from cartridges and refill bottles.

Research has found that some e-cigarettes contain chemicals other than nicotine and propylene glycol or glycerin. Tests on some e-cigarettes have found small amounts of nitrosamines, formaldehyde (both cancer-causing chemicals), acetaldehyde and acrolein (toxins) in the vapour or liquid. These are all chemicals found in tobacco smoke, at far higher levels.

Given reports of malfunctions, we'd like to see these products regulated to help ensure that the mechanical components in the device are safe and reliable, and deliver consistent doses of controlled chemical contents.

Who uses e-cigarettes and why?

E-cigarette manufacturers aren't yet allowed to market their products as quitting aids, as they haven't been through the strict tests needed to see how effective they are.

Some research suggests that smokers are already using them

to help give up and we want to see much more research to be sure if e-cigarettes could be useful in helping smokers quit (or cut down) smoking.

So we need to know more about how people use e-cigarettes, and why. For example:

⇨ How many people are using them to cut down their cigarette consumption, or to try to quit entirely?

⇨ Are people using e-cigarettes in combination with smoking, for example to 'get round' smoke-free laws?

⇨ If so, what impact does such 'dual use' mean for their future attempts to quit? Are they more or less likely?

⇨ Are smokers who may have otherwise successfully conquered their nicotine addiction more likely to stay on e-cigarettes (and thus addicted to nicotine) long term, if they start using them?

More research to answer such questions is needed to understand the long-term impacts of using e-cigarettes.

Effects on tobacco smoking?

One of the effects of decades of legislation against tobacco is to make smoking less socially acceptable, as more people are aware of the health risks and it has become more difficult to smoke in public. But the UK's smoke-free legislation doesn't cover e-cigarettes. So we also need to consider whether using e-cigarettes in places where tobacco smoking is now banned might make smoking more acceptable again.

Likewise, e-cigarettes aren't covered by the UK's ban on tobacco advertising. So e-cigarettes are marketed all over the place, and even promoted by celebrities and at celebrity events – techniques barred to the tobacco industry since 2003. It's important to look at whether e-cigarettes could serve as a 'gateway' to smoking

traditional cigarettes – by ex-smokers, non-smokers and, most importantly, children.

More than 200,000 under 16s start smoking in the UK every year, so protecting children from the dangers of smoking is a top priority for us. We need to find out more about whether e-cigarettes are attractive to children (particularly given the appealing flavourings and heavy advertising involving celebrities), and whether this will affect the number of children who subsequently take up smoking.

Tobacco industry involvement

Over the last few years, the tobacco industry has become heavily involved in selling e-cigarettes – a move that is seen by some as an 'insurance policy' against future potential losses in cigarette sales. This raises many issues around conflicts of interest and the role, if any, of the tobacco industry in public health.

The World Health Organisation's Framework Convention on Tobacco Control (FCTC) is a global public health treaty set up to provide a united response to the tobacco epidemic. Part of the FCTC aims to prevent tobacco industry interference and there are concerns this will be weakened by the industry's entry into the e-cigarette market and that this may simply be another tactic to keep profits high.

Next steps

Today's report by Stirling University will help guide future research and ultimately answer questions about potential benefits and harms of e-cigarettes. A comprehensive report by the French Office for Smoking

Prevention (OFT) has also just been published, which recommends a strict approach to marketing among other proposals.

In 2010, the Medicines and Healthcare Products Regulatory Agency (MHRA), which regulates all medicines and medical devices in the UK, asked for feedback on how to regulate new nicotine-containing products (including e-cigarettes).

We told them that we think such regulation will help address questions around the safety and effectiveness of e-cigarettes. The MHRA response to this consultation is expected imminently, along with results of the research they undertook to inform their decision.

Similarly, the National Institute for Health and Care Excellence (NICE) is due to publish new guidelines on tobacco harm reduction approaches to smoking, which may have implications for e-cigarettes. (Update: these guidelines are now published and do not include e-cigarettes.)

Quitting smoking is still the single most important thing smokers can do to for their health. We hope that the NICE guidance and the upcoming MHRA announcement will help provide smokers with the information and advice that they need to achieve this. And Cancer Research UK looks forward to working with others to deliver the research needed to inform the development of effective policies to support them.

11/06/13: this post was updated in response to the publication of NICE guidelines on tobacco harm reduction.

30 May 2013

⇨ The above information is reprinted with kind permission from Cancer Research UK. Please visit www.cancerresearchuk.org for further information.

Watch out, e-cigarette smokers – you're inhaling the unknown

Not only are these products not tested and regulated like proper medications – they are being targeted at the young.

By Tom Riddington

Electronic cigarettes sound fantastic. Rather than fill your lungs with tar, they deliver a vapour of nicotine to satisfy your craving, without the nasty side effects. They are popularly perceived as the safe alternative to cigarettes, a harmless way to get a nicotine hit. No wonder 700,000 people were using e-cigarettes in the UK last year, with that figure set to rise to over a million by the end of 2013.

Doctors are desperate to drive down the £5 billion a year that smoking-related illness costs the NHS. Anything that could help smokers quit would be welcomed. But e-cigarettes aren't a medicine. There's a reason you buy them from a newsagent rather than get them on prescription. E-cigarettes may look legitimate, but they haven't been through the same stringent safety checks as medicated nicotine-replacement therapies.

I want to be certain I'm giving the right advice to patients when they ask about e-cigarettes, not unwittingly jeopardising their health. Hardened smokers trying to quit are using them like prescription drugs, but they don't have any of the same safeguards. E-cigarettes are masquerading as medications – so let's subject them to the same scrutiny.

A quick search of medical journal archives reveals about 200 references to electronic cigarettes over the past five years. These products are relatively new, so there are no long-term studies on the effects of using them regularly. Instead, research is focused on what is being delivered to smokers' lungs in addition to nicotine.

The US Food and Drug Administration analysed the components of e-cigarette cartridges in 2009. They identified trace levels of tobacco-specific nitrosamines (TSNAs) – cancer-causing compounds commonly found in traditional cigarettes, albeit at a much lower concentration.

Although concerning, this isn't a huge surprise – similar levels are found in nicotine patches. But the FDA also found diethylene glycol, a component of antifreeze and brake fluids. Classed as a poison by the World Health Organization, at high enough quantities it can cause kidney damage, nerve dysfunction and respiratory failure.

In March 2013, researchers from the University of California examined in detail the aerosol contents of e-cigarettes. They found particles of silver, iron, aluminium and silicate, and nanoparticles of tin, chromium and nickel. The researchers noted that concentrations of these elements 'were higher than or equal to the corresponding concentrations in conventional cigarette smoke', and that 'many of the elements identified in [e-cigarette] aerosol are known to cause respiratory distress and disease'.

Other papers concentrate on the social effects of introducing a highly addictive drug to a new audience. *The Journal of Adolescent Health* identified e-cigarette ad campaigns that disproportionately appeal to a younger market, including 'celebrity endorsements, trendy/fashionable imagery, and fruit, candy and alcohol flavours'.

A comparison can be drawn with alcopops, and there are concerns that awareness of e-cigarettes is far greater among adolescents than among the general population. Instead of being an opportunity for current smokers to step down to something less harmful, they could be a gateway into smoking for young people who would not otherwise try cigarettes.

Some commentators have been sceptical about doctors' reticence to embrace e-cigarettes. Although I strongly encourage smokers to quit, I'm not comfortable advocating an unregulated, unlicensed consumer product that is marketing itself as a medicine. It has an unsettling similarity to when some doctors encouraged smoking for health before the damage of cigarettes was fully understood.

With a little research, it is clear that we do not know the risks of using e-cigarettes long-term, and the potential for harm is significant. Until the same regulations as other nicotine replacements are imposed, e-cigarettes should be considered a snake-oil gimmick that could get a new generation hooked on nicotine before their first smoke.

3 April 2013

⇨ The above information is reprinted with kind permission from *The Guardian*. Please visit www.guardian.co.uk for further information.

Passive smoking

You don't need to be a smoker to suffer the health effects of smoking. The smoker only inhales about 15% of the smoke from a cigarette. The other 85% is absorbed into the atmosphere or inhaled by other people. Second-hand smoke becomes invisible and odourless – this means you can't see or smell it. Breathing in this smoke is called passive smoking.

Health risks

Passive smokers face the same health risks smokers do. In the short term this can be:

⇨ sore eyes

⇨ headache

⇨ feeling sick and dizzy

⇨ a reduction of the flow of blood to the heart.

The long-term health risks include:

⇨ increased risk of heart disease

⇨ lung cancer

⇨ heart attacks and strokes.

Who it affects the most

Children

Children are in particular danger from passive smoking because they have smaller and weaker lungs. Babies are more likely to die from cot death. They are also more likely to develop chest infections, ear infections and asthma.

Pets

When you smoke you also put the health of your pets at risk. They have much smaller lungs than people do. This makes them more likely to have chest problems and it has also been linked to cancer in animals.

Your friends

When you smoke, it's not just your health that is at risk but also the health of your nearest and dearest. It's worth having a think about that when you smoke around them.

2 November 2012

⇨ The above information is reprinted with kind permission from Young Scot. Please visit www.youngscot. org for further information.

© *Young Scot 2014*

E-cigarettes 'could encourage young people to take up smoking', says research

By Jessica Elgot

E-cigarettes smoked by young people could lead to them picking up regular cigarettes, new research has claimed.

The study by the Health Equalities Group and the Centre for Public Health at Liverpool John Moores University suggests that claims by manufacturers that e-cigarettes prevent heavier smoking of tobacco are not necessarily true, with teenagers seeing them as different things.

The report's participants said e-cigarette use is becoming more common among young people who have never smoked traditional tobacco cigarettes, but the figures suggest the actual number is still very low. Around one in 40 e-cigarette smokers have never smoked tobacco.

'This behaviour was criticised by both smokers and non-smokers, who believed that e-cigarette use could easily lead on to smoking and even other substance use behaviours,' the report said.

'For many young people, e-cigarette use (particularly when tried for the first time) was associated with social gatherings and alcohol consumption.'

'This is particularly concerning given that the safety of e-cigarettes has not yet been thoroughly scientifically evaluated. It is clear that urgent action is needed to educate and protect young people,' said Robin Ireland, Chief Executive of Health Equalities Group.

Professor Karen Hughes, the lead author of the research, warned that use of the e-cigarette was growing rapidly.

The research was done through a series of focus groups conducted in schools, community groups and youth services as well as detailed quantitative research.

'Although some older adolescents appeared to associate e-cigarette use with smoking cessation, generally young people viewed e-cigarettes as a product in their own right, suggesting that many young people use them simply for the sake of it, for fun, or to try something new,' she said.

Guidance should be developed for schools and youth services to provide them with the tools they need to talk to young people about e-cigarette use and advice on developing policies addressing their use, the report said.

Amanda Sandford, the research manager at anti-smoking campaign ASH told *HuffPost UK*: 'This study supports the ASH finding that even trying an e-cigarette among children who have never smoked is extremely rare.'

2 April 2014

⇨ The above information is reprinted with kind permission from *Huffington Post UK*. Please visit www.huffingtonpost.co.uk.

© *2014 AOL (UK) Limited*

New film ignites the dangers of third-hand smoke

The dangers of smoking tobacco and the damage 'third-hand' smoke can cause have been documented in a new animation film.

Alarmed at the fact many people are unaware of the adverse effects of the habit, University of Sunderland student Satyajit Roy has made a film and it is now on show at the University's MA Design Degree Show 2013.

The 26-year-old was inspired to make the film, *Breath of Addiction*, after he encountered third-hand smoke himself due to his asthma condition. The Masters student, from India, has a passion to educate people about health and safety in his films. He hopes more people can now understand the dangers of smoking in the company of others.

Third-hand smoke is created by tobacco smoke lingering after a cigarette has been extinguished. It is called 'third-hand' because it is created once second-hand smoke has disappeared. It particularly clings to fabrics and people can be exposed to particles through inhalation, ingestion or skin contact.

Third-hand smoke is thought to be particularly dangerous to young children because they are more likely to crawl on the floor and eat from their hands without washing them first, ingesting the toxins into their system.

The short three-minute film explores and analyses the awareness of the problem and how it can cause damage. It shows a father smoking in the house and how the smoke stays on his body and seriously damages his daughter's health, before damaging his own.

Satyajit said: 'After doing extensive research I realised that a large number of the British population is unaware of the adverse affects of third-hand smoke. Therefore I decided to make this film in order to raise awareness. I hope that my film has a powerful impact on the minds of people and after seeing it they take the necessary measures to prevent the hazards of third-hand smoke.

'I'm an asthmatic sufferer and when I smell cigarette smoke I suffer a great deal. During the research I was shocked at how most people are affected but little is known about third-hand smoke and how it can affect people. It is quite a new term and not many people know about it so I wanted to make something to increase the awareness of the damage smoking can cause, even when you're not actually smoking.'

Satyajit studied biology and 3D animation in his native India before coming to the University of Sunderland to study his MA in animation and design. He now hopes after completing his MA he can work in the medical world to help raise the awareness of illnesses and medical conditions.

The Degree Show is exhibiting pieces of work from the MA animation and design, MA design studies, MA illustration and design and MA design: multimedia and graphics studies courses.

Dr Manny Ling, a senior lecturer in design said: 'I am delighted with the quality of the work this year. The MA design students have worked extremely hard to achieve their final outcomes. The works range from designing a single world currency to promoting better awareness for 'Empty Nest Syndrome' for old people. The quality of the work and the depth of engagement are exemplary.'

The exhibition is open until Friday, 4 October, between 10am and 5pm, and is at the Design Centre Gallery at the University of Sunderland City Campus, Chester Road.

18 September 2013

⇨ The above information is reprinted with kind permission from the University of Sunderland. Please visit www.sunderland.ac.uk for further information.

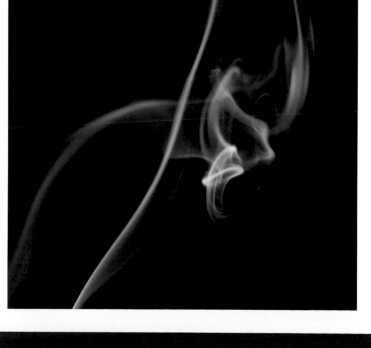

Brits unaware of signs of lung cancer

More than one in five people are unable to name any symptoms of the world's biggest cancer killer, according to a survey published to mark the start of Lung Cancer Awareness Month.

The research, which was carried out by Ipsos MORI on behalf of the Global Lung Cancer Coalition, investigated awareness of the symptoms of lung cancer and smoking prevalence in 21 countries.

Researchers found that across all the countries, 22% of people surveyed admitted they could not name any symptoms of the disease, which claims the lives of 1.37 million people globally every year[1].

In Britain, the survey found that;

⇨ one in five (20%) people were current smokers and those aged 65 or older were more likely to be former smokers than other age groups (39% vs. 21% on average);

⇨ when asked to identify the symptoms of lung cancer, breathlessness and a cough were the most commonly stated symptoms (46% and 43%), in line with many other countries surveyed;

⇨ current smokers were less aware of the symptoms of lung cancer than former smokers and people who had never smoked regularly (22% of smokers, 9% of former smokers and 15% of people who had never smoked don't know any).

The Global Lung Cancer Coalition's British members include the British Lung Foundation, the National Lung Cancer Forum for Nurses and the Roy Castle Lung Cancer Foundation.

Paula Chadwick, chief executive of Roy Castle Lung Cancer Foundation, said: 'The majority of people know that a lump in their breast or their testicles can be a sign of cancer.

'However, awareness of the symptoms of lung cancer is exceptionally low despite it being the biggest cancer killer.

'The earlier people are diagnosed, the more chance they can receive treatment and the more lives that can be saved.'

Dr Penny Woods, chief executive of the British Lung Foundation, said:

'With lung cancer killing more than any other cancer worldwide, it is concerning that there is still such a lack of lung cancer awareness, especially among smokers. Two out of every five lung cancer diagnoses are made when patients are admitted to A&E but most cases should be detectable long before this stage.

'It is vital that people become more aware of their lung health and the symptoms of lung cancer – this could make a huge difference in detecting lung cancer at an early stage and increasing the chances of successful treatment.

'Smoking causes more than 80% of lung cancers so it is also important that we continue to support smokers to quit whilst exploring new ways of discouraging young people from taking it up in the first place, such as introducing standardised packaging for all tobacco products.'

Diana Borthwick, from the National Lung Cancer Forum for Nurses, said: 'This survey demonstrates that more work needs to be done around raising awareness nationally as well as globally.

'By increasing awareness and raising the profile of lung cancer we may hope to make the public more aware of the symptoms of lung cancer so they can seek help at an earlier stage.'

The report found lack of awareness of lung cancer symptoms varied between different countries.

Egyptian (48%), Argentinian (42%), Mexican (35%) and Portuguese (33%) respondents are most likely to say they couldn't name any symptoms. At the other end of the spectrum, fewer than one in ten French (7%) and Irish (9%) people are unable to name any symptoms.

Overall, breathlessness was the most commonly identified symptom (41% of respondents mentioned it spontaneously on average across the countries) but a similar proportion identified a cough or coughing (39% on average across the countries). Others mentioned more specific types of coughing such as coughing blood or a cough that gets worse.

In Australia and Great Britain, current smokers are less aware of the symptoms of lung cancer than former smokers and people who have never smoked. In three countries (France, Ireland and Portugal), current smokers appear to have greater awareness of potential symptoms.

⇨ The above information is reprinted with kind permission from The Roy Castle Lung Cancer Foundation. Please visit www.roycastle.org for further information.

© The Roy Castle Lung Cancer Foundation 2014

1 This is based on 2008 data – the latest available. http://globocan.iarc.fr/factsheet.asp

Health check: how harmful is social smoking?

THE CONVERSATION

An article from The Conversation.

By Ian Olver, Clinical Professor of Oncology at Cancer Council Australia

If you only light up when you're drinking or out with friends, you probably don't identify as a smoker or consider the health impact of the occasional fag. Social smokers don't usually smoke every day but consume a low level of tobacco over a long period.

30 years ago, the tobacco industry studied social smokers because they wanted to promote the 'social benefits' of smoking. They discovered many were motivated to achieve a certain image or wanted help relaxing and de-stressing. The companies tried to tap into this market, offering smaller pack sizes and promoting cigarettes which were claimed to be safer and non-habit forming; which of course was nonsense.

Modern social smokers are typically younger, better educated and more affluent than other smokers and often smoke to gain acceptance among their social group, rather than in response to a craving for nicotine.

It's difficult to know the percentage of smokers who currently fall into the social smoker category because this group isn't explicitly counted. But among Australians over the age of 14, 15.1% smoke daily, 1.5% weekly and 1.4% less-than weekly. It's unclear whether rates of social smoking in Australia are changing, but American figures suggest social smoking is on the rise.

Although social smokers may feel less vulnerable to harm than heavier smokers, they are still likely to suffer from smoking-related respiratory disease, heart attack, stroke and cancer. Smoking as little as one to four cigarettes each day triples your risk of heart disease and lung cancer.

With more than 60 known carcinogens in cigarette smoke, the campaign slogan that every cigarette is doing you damage is true: the more you smoke, the greater your risk. And although social smokers only smoke occasionally, they may indulge in binge smoking on those occasions.

Because nicotine is so addictive, social smokers can quickly become more regular, addicted smokers. Before long, they're buying their own cigarettes, starting to smoke alone and wake in the morning craving a cigarette.

It is also very difficult for regular smokers to decrease consumption – to become a social smoker – because nicotine is so addictive.

The solution?
Quit completely

When social smokers quit, they may avoid the withdrawal symptoms suffered by those addicted to nicotine. So the quit techniques for regular daily smokers may not apply.

Tobacco industry research has shown that social smokers tend to be more concerned than regular smokers about second-hand smoke affecting non-smokers and that these concerns could influence their smoking behaviour and decision to quit. After all, there's nothing social about second-hand smoke.

If you are a social smoker wanting to quit, try enlisting friends to dissuade you from lighting up in social situations. If you smoke when you drink alcohol, cutting back on booze may also help.

When you quit smoking, some of the improvements commence within hours, but the reduction in the risk of serious disease will take many years.

Within the first six hours, the heart rate decreases and blood pressure drops. Most of the nicotine is cleared in the first day.

With a week, the sense of taste and smell improve and lungs begin to clear. The symptoms of a cough and wheeze progressively improve over the first year.

After ten years, the risk of lung cancer is lower than if the individual had continued smoking and by 15 years the risk of heart attack and stroke returns to those of someone who has never smoked.

6 January 2014

⇨ The above information is reprinted with kind permission from The Conversation. Please visit www.theconversation.com for further information.

The impact of smoking in films on young people

Introduction

There is a growing body of evidence from studies in the UK, the USA and elsewhere which shows that exposing young audiences to on-screen smoking and tobacco imagery has a strong impact on smoking initiation.

A study of ten- to 14-year-olds that had never smoked found that those most exposed to film smoking were more than four times more likely to take up smoking than those with least exposure. Other findings have revealed that adolescents whose favourite film stars smoke on screen are more likely to have tried smoking.

For young people there is no safe level of exposure to on-screen smoking and health experts across the globe are calling for more to be done to reduce or eliminate youth exposure to on-screen smoking to reduce smoking levels amongst young people.

Examples of tobacco imagery in films popular in the UK

⇨ Glenn Close playing Cruella de Vil in the popular children's film *101 Dalmatians* (1996) (BBFC Universal)

⇨ Sigourney Weaver playing grace in the popular film *Avatar* (2009) (BBFC 12A)

⇨ Rene Zellweger as Bridget Jones in *Bridget Jones: The Edge of Reason* (2004) (BBFC 15)

⇨ Bérénice Marlohe as Severine in *Skyfall* (2012) (BBFC 12A).

Making the case

Scientific evidence

Tobacco companies are not alone in concluding that films sell smoking. Science from a dozen countries shows tobacco on-screen content is proven to exert a lasting harmful effect on the behaviour of large numbers of young people. The US Surgeon General, National Cancer Institute and the WHO have all concluded that there is a casual relationship between exposure to smoking on screen and youth smoking initiation.

In 2012, the USA Center for Disease Control and Prevention (CDC) reported that tobacco incidents per movie rated G, PG and PG13 increased 34 per cent in 2011 and that in-theatre tobacco impression delivered by youth-rated films doubled over 2010. This supports the 2012 USA Surgeon General report which stated that nearly a third of top grossing films produced for children – those with ratings of G, PG or PG13 – have contained images of smoking.

Research from the University of Bristol (ALSPAC) in 2011 revealed that 15-year-olds who saw the most films showing smoking were 73 per cent more likely to have tried a cigarette than those exposed to the least.

Commercial history

There is solid documentary evidence that US film productions, of the kind that dominate UK screens, have had a long history of collaborating with the tobacco industry to promote smoking and tobacco brands.

Internal tobacco industry documents from the 1920s and 30s identified endorsement contracts between the tobacco industry and film stars and studies, as well as revealing the cross-promotional value of these campaigns.

There is also evidence that paid-for tobacco product placements persisted at least as far as the 1990s. After 1970, when tobacco advertising was banned from the US airwaves, major tobacco companies launched systematic product placement campaigns, touching hundreds of mainstream films.

Unique problem

It is the smoking depiction that prompts adolescents to smoke, not other characteristics of films such as sex, alcohol or violence which are routinely subject to age-classification. The harms caused by on-screen smoking need to be recognised and action taken to tackle the impacts.

Results

A recent study by the UKCTAS which tracked the occurrence of tobacco imagery and tobacco branding in the highest 15 grossing films at the UK

cinema box office in each year from 1989 to 2011 found:

⇨ Tobacco was depicted in 70% of all films

⇨ Over half (56%) of films that contained tobacco were rated by the British Board of Film Classification (BBFC) as suitable for viewing by those aged under 15

⇨ 92% were rated suitable for those aged under 18

⇨ Brand appearance was more than twice as likely to occur in films originating wholly, or partly from the UK (36%), when compared to those from the US (20%)

⇨ Brands appeared in 9% of all films, and the most commonly depicted brands were Marlboro and Silk Cut.

Evidence-based solutions to tackling smoking on the big screen

To counter this, public health groups have been working together to urge film makers and regulators to take tobacco out of films. They have developed four 'smokefree movie policies' which have been endorsed by health authorities worldwide:

⇨ play an effective anti-tobacco advert before any film with tobacco imagery is shown in cinemas

⇨ have producers confirm that no one associated with a film production received any subsidisation for using or displaying tobacco imagery

⇨ eliminate tobacco imagery in films altogether

⇨ assign an adult rating (e.g. 18) to films made with tobacco content, except if it reflects the consequences of tobacco use or is necessary for historical accuracy.

References

1. Lyons A, McNeill, A, Chen, Y, & Britton, J. *Tobacco and tobacco branding in films popular in the UK 1989-2008*. Thorax 2010;65:417-22

2. Millett C, Glantz SA (2010) *Assigning an 18 rating to tobacco imagery is essential to reduce youth smoking (editorial)*. Thorax http://thorax.bmj.com/content/65/5/377.full 65:377-378

3. Tickle J, Sargent, JD, Dalton, MA, Beach, ML, & Heatherton, TF. *Favourite movie stars, their tobacco use in contemporary movies, and its association with adolescent smoking*. Tobacco Control 2001;10:16-22

4. Dalton M, Sargent, JD, Beach, ML, Titus-Ernstoff, L, Gibson, JJ, Ahrens, MB, Tickle, JJ, & Heatherton, TF. *Effect of viewing smoking in movies on adolescent smoking initiation: a cohort study*. Lancet 2003;362:281-5.

5. U.S. Department of Health and Human Services. *Preventing tobacco use among youth and young adults: A report of the Surgeon General*. Rockville, MD: U.S. Department of Health and Human Services 2012

6. The National Cancer Institute. *The Role of the Media in Promoting and reducing Tobacco Use. Tobacco Control Monograph No. 19*. U.S. Department of Health and Human Services National Institutes of Health, 2008

7. World Health Organization (WHO). *Smoke-free movies: From evidence to action*. World Health Organisation Geneva 2009:1-29

8. Waylen A, Leary, SD, Ness, AR, Tanski, SE, & Sargent, JD. *Cross sectional association between smoking depictions in films and adolescent tobacco use nested in a British cohort study*. Thorax 2011;66:856-61

9. Lum K, Polansky, JR, Jackler, RK, & Glantz, SA. *Signed, sealed and delivered: 'Big Tobacco' in Hollywood, 1927-1951*. Tobacco Control 2008;17:313-23

10. Mekemson C, & Glantz SA. *How the tobacco industry built its relationship with Hollywood*. Tobacco Control 2002;11 Suppl 1:I81-91

11. James D. Sargent, Susanne Tanski and Mike Stoolmiller. *Influence of Motion Picture Rating on Adolescent Response to Movie Smoking*. Pediatrics; July 2012; http://pediatrics.aappublications.org/content/early/2012/07/03/peds.2011-1787

12. Including UKCTCAS; ASH; *Tobacco Free Futures*; Legacy (USA); Smoke Free Movies (USA)

13. Lyons, A. & Britton, J. (2013). *Conference poster: A content analysis of tobacco and alcohol in popular UK films, an update*. The Lancet. Volume 382, Page S66. (29 November 2013) Available from: http://www.thelancet.com/journals/lancet/article/PIIS0140-6736(13)62491-5/abstract

⇨ The above information is reprinted with kind permission from Tobacco Free Futures. Please visit www.tobaccofreefutures.org for further information.

More than 200,000 UK children start smoking every year

Around 207,000 children aged 11–15 start smoking in the UK every year according to research published in March 2013.

This means that nearly 570 children are lighting up and becoming smokers for the first time every day.

The new Cancer Research UK figures show this number has jumped by an extra 50,000 from the previous year, when 157,000 started smoking.

Analysis of the data showed that the 2010 figure was unusually low and this most recent figure is similar to the numbers seen in the late 2000s.

Around 27 per cent of all under-16s have tried smoking at least once – equivalent to one million children. Eight out of ten adult smokers start before they turn 19.

And the figures show that older children smoke more than younger ones.

A survey among 12-year-olds in 2010 found none were regular smokers, one per cent smoked occasionally and two per cent said they used to smoke.

But a year later in 2011 among the same age group of children, now aged 13, two per cent were found to smoke regularly, four per cent smoked occasionally and three per cent said they used to smoke.

Half of all long-term smokers will die from tobacco-related illness. Around 100,000 people are killed by smoking in the UK each year.

With so many children starting to smoke each year, Cancer Research UK is urging the Government to commit to plain, standardised packaging of tobacco. Research has shown that children find the plain packs less appealing and are less likely to be misled by the sophisticated marketing techniques designed to make smoking attractive to youngsters.

A public consultation on the future of tobacco packaging closed in August 2012 and there has been no decision announced from the Government on whether this will proceed.

Sarah Woolnough, Cancer Research UK's executive director of policy and information, said: 'With such a large number of youngsters starting to smoke every year, urgent action is needed to tackle the devastation caused by tobacco. Replacing slick, brightly coloured packs that appeal to children with standard packs displaying prominent health warnings, is a vital part of efforts to protect health. Reducing the appeal of cigarettes with plain, standardised packs will give millions of children one less reason to start smoking.

'These figures underline the importance of sustained action to discourage young people from starting. Smoking kills and is responsible for at least 14 different types of cancer. Standardised packaging is popular with the public and will help protect children. We urge the Government to show their commitment to health and introduce plain, standardised packs as soon as possible.'

22 March 2013

⇨ The above information is reprinted with kind permission from Cancer Research UK. Please visit www.cancerresearchuk.org for further information.

THIS PLAIN PACKET LOOK SUCKS – I'm OUTTA HERE!

Quitting and trends

Quitting is the best thing you'll ever do

Stopping smoking can make a drastic improvement to your lifestyle and health in ways you might not expect. Once you stop smoking, some of the benefits are immediate and some are longer-term.

For you

⇨ You will save money – the average smoker has 13 cigarettes a day, which works out as 364 cigarettes a month. That's £141 a month and £1,696 a year that you could be saving by not smoking.

⇨ Your sense of taste will return and you will enjoy the taste of food more.

⇨ Your breathing and general fitness will improve.

⇨ The appearance of your skin and teeth will improve.

⇨ You'll be more confident in social situations because you won't smell of stale smoke any more.

⇨ Your fertility levels will improve, along with your chances of having a healthy pregnancy and baby.

There are also real benefits for your family and friends

⇨ You will protect the health of those around you by not exposing them to second-hand smoke, however careful you think you are being.

⇨ You will reduce the chances of your children suffering from bronchitis, pneumonia, asthma attacks, meningitis and ear infections.

⇨ The above information is reprinted with kind permission from the NHS. Please visit www.nhs.uk for further information.

© NHS 2014

> **'I've been stopped for 17 weeks now. I'm proud of myself and the best thing is being able to do more exercise and not waking up with a sore chest anymore.'**
>
> *Sian-Marie, 20-30 a day for 13 years*

Find out how quickly you'll notice the benefits of stopping

After 20 minutes
Blood pressure and pulse rate return to normal.

After 8 hours
Nicotine and carbon monoxide levels in blood reduce by half and oxygen levels return to normal.

After 48 hours
Carbon monoxide will be eliminated from the body. Lungs start to clear out mucus and other smoking debris.

After 48 hours
There is no nicotine in the body. Ability to taste and smell is greatly improved.

After 72 hours
Breathing becomes easier. Bronchial tubes begin to relax and energy levels increase.

After 2–12 weeks
Your circulation improves.

After 3–9 months
Coughs, wheezing and breathing problems improve as lung function increases by up to 10%.

After 5 years
Risk of heart attacks falls to about half compared with a person who is still smoking.

After 10 years
Risk of lung cancer falls to half that of a smoker. Risk of heart attack falls to the same as someone who has never smoked.

Source: NHS Choices 2012

Doctors back denial of treatment for smokers and the obese

Survey finds 54% of doctors think the NHS should have the right to withhold non-emergency treatment.

By Denis Campbell, health correspondent

A majority of doctors support measures to deny treatment to smokers and the obese, according to a survey that has sparked a row over the NHS's growing use of 'lifestyle rationing'.

Some 54% of doctors who took part said the NHS should have the right to withhold non-emergency treatment from patients who do not lose weight or stop smoking. Some medics believe unhealthy behaviour can make procedures less likely to work, and that the service is not obliged to devote scarce resources to them.

However, senior doctors and patient groups have voiced alarm at what they call 'blackmailing' of the sick, and denial of their human rights.

Doctors.net.uk, a professional networking site, found that 593 (54%) of the 1,096 doctors who took part in the self-selecting survey answered yes when asked: 'Should the NHS be allowed to refuse non-emergency treatments to patients unless they lose weight or stop smoking?'

One doctor said that denying in-vitro fertilisation to childless women who smoked was justified because it was only half as successful for them. Another said the NHS was right to expect an obese patient or alcoholic to change their behaviour before they underwent liver transplant surgery.

Dr Tim Ringrose, Doctors.net.uk's chief executive, said the findings represented a significant shift in doctors' thinking brought on by the NHS in England's need to save £20 billion by 2015. 'This might appear to be only a slim majority of doctors in favour of limiting treatment to some patients who fail to look after themselves, but it represents a tectonic shift for a profession that has always sought to provide free healthcare from the cradle to the grave,' he said.

Smokers and obese people are already being denied operations such as IVF, breast reconstructions and a new hip or knee in some parts of England. The medical magazine *Pulse* last month found that 25 of 91 primary care trusts (PCTs) had introduced treatment bans for those groups since April 2011.

Bedfordshire PCT, for example, decided to withhold hip and knee surgery from obese patients until they had slimmed down by 10% or had a body mass index of under 35. Similarly, North Essex PCT obliged obese people to lose 5% of their bodyweight and keep the pounds shed for at least six months before receiving treatment.

But Dr Clare Gerada, chair of the Royal College of General Practitioners, said the survey findings and trend towards 'lifestyle rationing' was 'very disturbing'.

She said: 'It's the deserving and undeserving sick idea. The NHS should deliver care according to need. There was no medical justification for such restrictions on smokers, as giving up nicotine would not necessarily enhance an operation's chances of success. Clearly, giving up smoking is a good thing. But blackmailing people by telling them that they have to give up isn't what doctors should be doing.'

Doctors should not back such bans unless there was 'overwhelming evidence' that stopping smoking reduces the patient's risk of suffering complications or dying, she said.

But obesity could merit such bans, Gerada said. 'Obesity is a different matter. Operating on a very fat person is more dangerous. Anaesthetically it's harder, the surgery is harder and the rehabilitation takes longer. So it's medically legitimate to withhold treatment from some very overweight people. But it should not be done for social reasons,' she said.

Tam Fry, spokesman for the National Obesity Forum, said doctors who back bans 'are totally out of order. There's no way that someone who is obese can be denied initial treatment by the NHS – that would be totally unjustified. There are many reasons why people are fat and gluttony is only one of them. The NHS should not be discriminating against fat people purely on the grounds of their fatness. That would be a denial of their basic human rights.'

The Royal College of Physicians, which represents hospital doctors, said it opposed the practice. 'Lifestyle rationing is creeping into the NHS. There are reported examples where treatments have been restricted by PCTs and we wouldn't agree with that,' said Professor John Saunders, chair of the college's ethics committees.

But he defended doctors' right to examine whether a patient's lifestyle might reduce the chances of a treatment succeeding. 'Some lifestyles will impact on the success of treatments; for example, if someone weighs 150kg, that may have an impact on the outcome.

'Lifestyles contribute to risk and sometimes they may make treatments too risky to undertake. But that's quite different to saying, "I'm not going to give you surgery because you smoke or are overweight'," said Saunders.

The Department of Health took a similar stance. 'There is no excuse to deny care on the basis of arbitrary blanket bans – the individual needs of patients must be taken into account,' said a spokeswoman.

'But there can be clinical reasons to ask someone to take action such as losing weight or stop smoking before surgery because the risk of surgery can become greater.'

Dr Mark Porter, chairman of the British Medical Association's consultants committee, blasted treatment bans as 'wholly unacceptable'. But he added: 'There are occasions where a doctor may advise an obese person to lose weight before surgery can safely go ahead. This is a clinical rather than a rationing decision.'

Dr Ringrose said: 'Perhaps it's time for the NHS to have a realistic discussion with UK taxpayers about what treatments it can continue to cover.'

29 April 2012

⇨ The above information is reprinted with kind permission from *The Guardian*. Please visit www.guardian.co.uk for further information.

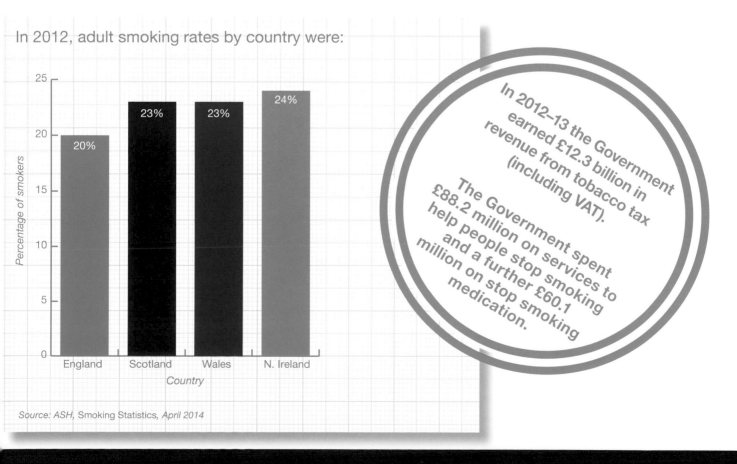

In 2012, adult smoking rates by country were:

Percentage of smokers

England 20%
Scotland 23%
Wales 23%
N. Ireland 24%

Country

Source: ASH, Smoking Statistics, April 2014

In 2012–13 the Government earned £12.3 billion in revenue from tobacco tax (including VAT).

The Government spent £88.2 million on services to help people stop smoking and a further £60.1 million on stop smoking medication.

Stop smoking services help 20,000 quit

England's NHS 'stop smoking services' have enabled at least 20,000 smokers to kick the habit in 2010/11 according to new research in the *British Medical Journal* and the number of smokers helped each year has more than tripled over that time period.

The number of smokers who used the service and set a quit date more than tripled from just over 227,000 in 2001/02 to nearly 788,000 in 2010/11. The total number of quitters who had not smoked for four weeks rose from just under 80,000 to almost 270,000.

The stop smoking services provide smokers with expert advice on how to stop together with discussion about the best options when it comes to stop smoking medicines. Smokers are followed up for at least four weeks following the quit date to help them through the most difficult period.

Until 2013, stop smoking services in England were provided through 151 primary care trusts. Since April 2013, local authorities hold the budget. Each local area can run its service as it wants but is encouraged to follow national guidance.

Eileen Streets, director of tobacco control at Roy Castle Lung Cancer Foundation, said: 'This report emphasises the importance of stop smoking services in tackling health inequalities and improving the health of the nation.

'It has already been proven how cost effective stop smoking support is given that one in two smokers will die of a smoking related disease.'

Alison Cox, Cancer Research UK's head of tobacco policy, said: 'With local authorities now in charge of this area of public health, these findings provide reassurance that stop smoking services are effective and provide value for money in reducing the deadly toll from tobacco. A close watch needs to be kept on the local provision of these services. Reduced support to smokers would be a very bad outcome of the NHS restructure as it would increase health inequalities, and could ultimately cost lives.'

Researchers analysed data from when the services began in earnest in 2001 to 2011, and examined how many people were successful at stopping smoking long term after using the service compared with what would have been expected if they had just received a prescription from their doctor for a stop smoking medicine. The researchers used known relapse rates after four weeks to estimate long-term quit rates in service users.

The services were also successful in reaching disadvantaged smokers with 54 per cent of quitters in 2010/11 being eligible for free prescriptions.

While the overall picture is positive, the research found large variation in performance across local services with some doing more than twice as well as others.

Professor Robert West, Cancer Research UK Director of Tobacco Research at University College London led the research, he said: "England's stop smoking services have led the world and saved lives more cost-effectively than just about any other area of the NHS – a real success story. However, there is clearly room for improvement and a need to bring the poorer performing services up to standard.'

Alison Cox added: 'Tobacco is a lethal product that kills half of all long-term smokers, so helping smokers to quit is an incredibly important job. The quality of the services are world leading and this research shows just how successful they've been.'

For free help and advice to quit smoking visit https://healthunlocked.com/quitsupport.

⇨ The above information is reprinted with kind permission from The Roy Castle Lung Cancer Foundation. Please visit www.roycastle.org for further information.

Smoke and mirrors

Vain smokers are more concerned about the effects cigarettes have on their looks than their health, research has revealed.

Experts found despite the potentially fatal long-term consequences of lighting up regularly, a large percentage still find skin wrinkles and yellow teeth more troubling than lung damage.

The study also found more than half of smokers either have, or are planning to quit over fears about the damage it is doing to their appearance.

But the in-depth findings by electronic cigarette brand VIP found one in seven admitted they would be more likely to give up the cigarettes if they noticed an effect on how they looked, rather than because their health was suffering.

This New Year, over a quarter admitted this was the reason they have decided to quit tobacco for good.

Dave Levin, co-owner of VIP said: 'The health effects of smoking are well documented, but people are less aware that cigarettes can also damage your looks.

'During our research three quarters of smokers said that their habit had caused deterioration to their looks and it was this, more than their health, that concerned them.'

Top ten effects smokers worry about cigarettes having on their looks

1. Yellowing teeth
2. Bad breath
3. General odour from smoke
4. An increase in wrinkles
5. An increase in fine lines
6. Yellowing nails/fingers
7. Missing teeth
8. Wrinkly mouth/lips
9. Bad skin
10. Discoloured/ashen skin

'While the health issues caused by smoking are so widely advertised, they aren't always as easy to see or notice.

'But the effects on your appearance are something you can see every time you look at your reflection, whether it's deeper wrinkles, discoloured teeth or a sallow complexion.'

And the average smoker said that damage started to show around the age of 32.

A staggering 88 per cent even admitted they regret taking it up in the first place because it is now showing in their appearance.

Worryingly, the research also revealed that more than eight in ten admitted they are more likely to take notice of the effects of smoking they can actually see, such as yellow teeth and wrinkles, rather than what it is doing to their health and body internally.

Yellow teeth were named as the biggest concern with more than four in ten smokers saying they hated the effect cigarettes have had on their smile.

Bad breath, as well as the general odour that goes with being a smoker followed close behind, along with an increase in fine lines and wrinkles.

Stained and discoloured nails and fingers, wrinkled mouth and bad or ashen skin are also among the aspects of their appearance that smokers worry about.

One in three smokers has experienced somebody insulting them or pointing out the effects of tobacco directly to their face.

And four in ten spend more time on their beauty regime to try and compensate for the effects of the cigarettes.

Dave Levin added: 'During the Christmas period Public Health England launched its latest TV advertising campaign to

graphically demonstrate the health implications of tobacco. While we feel these messages are important and will resonate with some smokers, our research indicates that for many, vanity is also a key issue.

'VIP electronic cigarettes have been designed to offer a harm-reducing alternative to smokers. They are not only widely recognised by a number of leading health professionals as healthier than tobacco cigarettes, but they're also much kinder on our looks.

'Electronic cigarettes are free of the harmful toxins found in tobacco cigarettes which mean users can enjoy the great taste of VIP and stay looking good. What's more, because VIP electronic cigarettes are virtually odourless and smoke free, there are no lingering tobacco smells.'

⇨ The above information is reprinted with kind permission from VIP Electronic Cigarettes. Please visit www.vipecig.co.uk for further information.

© VIP Electronic Cigarettes 2014

Stoptober challenge reaches new high as country's biggest mass quit attempt

Brits could add 4,700 years to their lives and £34.5 million to their wallets.

Nearly a quarter of a million people in England and Wales turned their back on their cigarettes this month to reap the financial, social and health benefits from taking part in the mass 28-day stop smoking challenge, Stoptober.

Research shows that stopping smoking for 28 days can extend your life by up to one week if you remain smokefree [1]. The new ex-smokers across England and Wales are therefore celebrating their first steps towards a healthier, smokefree life, and if they succeed in quitting for good, they could collectively add as much as 4,700 years of life to the population [2].

However, taking part in Stoptober has delivered even more than the health benefits; there are major savings in time and money:

⇨ the average smoker has 13 cigarettes a day [3], which equates to 364 cigarettes every four weeks. Stoptober would have saved them £141 each over four weeks [4], and if they remain smokefree, they could save £423 by Christmas and £1,696 in a year. Collectively, if all Stoptober participants quit for the 28 days this month they would have saved over £34.5 million

⇨ with the average cigarette taking approximately four minutes to smoke [5], this Stoptober could have saved the average smoker over 24 hours by not smoking; and cumulatively Stoptober participants would have gained over 680 years in spare time.

Backed by a huge number of supporters – including celebrities, charities, sports clubs and stop smoking services – Stoptober has helped thousands of people try and stay free from cigarettes through support packs, a 28-day app, social media activities and tips and advice from a host of celebrity well-wishers.

Actress and singer Kelsey-Beth Crossley, took on the 28-day stop smoking challenge to improve her health and protect her singing voice. Commenting on her quit attempt, Kelsey-Beth said:

'I did find the 28 days a real challenge – especially to begin with – but knowing so many other people were going through the same thing was really motivating and encouraging.

'Well done to everyone who has managed to get through 28 days smokefree – long may it continue and good luck for the future.'

Joanne Eccles, 40 from Gateshead said:

'Completing the 28-day challenge is a massive triumph and I feel a real sense of achievement. It wasn't easy but all the support from friends and family really helped me along the way.

'What's even better is I have saved over £200 and now I am going to take the kids away for a weekend. I can't believe how much money I used to waste every month.'

Stoptober started on 1 October 2013 and ran for 28 days. Research shows that those who stop smoking for 28 days are five times more likely to stay smokefree. Last year saw over 160,000 people successfully complete the four-week challenge.

It is not too late to start your own 28-day challenge – for more information and to download the Stoptober app visit the Stoptober website (www.stoptober. smokefree.nhs.uk).

References

[1] University of Toronto: 21st Century Hazards of Smoking and Benefits of Cessation in the United States.

[2] Based on 245,000 people each gaining one week of life over a 28-day period, if they remain smokefree.

[3] Average daily consumption of 13 manufactured cigarettes per smoker (2011 General Lifestyle Survey).

[4] Based on £7.77 for a packet of cigarettes (Office of National Statistics, May 2013).

[5] Based on a Stoptober survey of 500 smokers in October 2012.

Notes

Stoptober started on 1 October and ran for 28 days and included TV and outdoor advertising, digital activity, posters, cards and in-pharmacy literature, roadshows and national and regional PR.

Public Health England's mission is to protect and improve the nation's health and to address inequalities through working with national and local government, the NHS, industry and the voluntary and community sector. PHE is an operationally autonomous executive agency of the Department of Health.

For more information on the biggest stop smoking challenge of its kind, search 'Stoptober' online.

29 October 2013

⇨ The above information is reprinted with kind permission from GOV.UK. For further information please visit www. gov.uk.

Public Health Committee MEPs toughen up plans to deter young people from smoking

A draft law to make smoking less attractive to the young by banning the use of 'characterised' flavours such as strawberry or menthol in tobacco products was backed by Public Health Committee MEPs on Wednesday. But they also amended the draft to require health warnings on every side of a cigarette pack and ban slim cigarettes and 'attractive' packaging.

'Smoking remains the leading cause of preventable death in the EU, killing around 700,000 people per year'

'The focus is to prevent the industry from recruiting new smokers among the young,' said Linda McAvan (S&D, UK) who is steering the legislation through Parliament. 'The smoking trend is down, as action by public authorities has reduced the number of smokers over the years. However, there is a worrying drift: 29% of young people smoke. The World Health Organization has shown that since 2005, the trend has been going up amongst young boys and girls in some countries,' she added.

The draft legislation was approved by 50 votes to 13, with eight abstentions.

'The labelling or packaging of any tobacco product must not suggest that a particular product is less harmful than others or has positive health or lifestyle effects'

Additives and flavours

The updated Tobacco Product Directive (TPD) will prohibit the use in tobacco products of additives and flavours that make a product more attractive, by imparting a characterising flavour, and also the use of vitamins, caffeine and taurine. Additives such as sugar that are essential for the manufacture of tobacco products would be permitted.

No misleading labelling

The labelling or packaging of any tobacco product must not suggest that a particular product is less harmful than others or has positive health or lifestyle effects. It should also not resemble a food or cosmetic product, MEPs say.

Health warnings

Packets and packaging of cigarettes, roll-your-own tobacco and water pipe tobacco should display health warnings on all sides of packets. These warnings should cover at least 75% of the external area of both the front and back surfaces, said the committee.

Ban slim cigarettes

'Slim' cigarettes, of a diameter of less than 7.5mm, and packets with less than 20 cigarettes should be banned, the report says. So-called 'lipstick packs' would also be banned.

Cross-border distance sales should be prohibited.

E-cigarettes

E-cigarettes may only be placed on the market under existing rules on medicinal products. However, 'given the potential of these products to aid with smoking cessation, Member States should ensure that they can be made available outside pharmacies,' MEPs say.

No more tar and nicotine info on packs

The tar, nicotine and carbon monoxide yields of cigarettes must henceforth be measured on the basis of referenced ISO standards, as existing indications displayed on cigarette packets have proven to be misleading, MEPs say. They therefore propose that no such information should be included on packs.

Combatting illegal trade

To reduce the volume of illicit tobacco products placed on the market, member states must ensure that all unit packets and outside transport packaging are marked with an identifier. This should make it possible to trace the shipment route from the manufacturer to the first retail outlet, say MEPs.

Background

12 years after the current directive came into force, smoking remains the leading cause of preventable death in the EU, killing around 700,000 people per year. Measures taken over the years to cut smoking have had an impact: in the past decade the number of smokers has fallen from nearly 40% in the EU 15 in 2002 to 28% in the EU 27 in 2012.

Next steps

The report will be put to a vote in plenary session this autumn, in Strasbourg.

10 July 2013

⇨ The above information is reprinted with kind permission from European Parliament. Please visit www.europarl.europa.eu for further information.

MPs vote in favour of banning smoking in cars with child passengers despite opposition

By Paul Vale

Parliament has opened the door for legislation that would prevent children from being exposed to second-hand smoke in cars following a vote in the Commons on Monday. The Health Secretary now has the power to impose a ban, despite opposition from some members of the Cabinet.

Labour introduced the amendment to the Children and Families Bill to the House of Lords, after which it went to the Commons for a free vote. Anti-smoking charities were quick to praise the move with Dr Penny Woods, chief executive of the British Lung Foundation, saying she was 'absolutely delighted that MPs have backed the ban on smoking in cars carrying children'.

Woods added: 'This could prove a great leap forward for the health of our nation's children. The introduction of a law that would help prevent hundreds of thousands of children from being exposed to second-hand smoke in the car is now within reach. With both Houses of Parliament having made their support for the ban clear, the onus is now on the Government to act accordingly and make this crucial child protection measure law at the earliest opportunity.'

More from the Press Association:

According to the British Lung Foundation, each week more than 400,000 children aged between 11–15 are exposed to second-hand smoke in a car. Research published by the organisation last year concluded that 185,000 children of the same age are exposed to smoke while in the family car on 'most days', if not every day.

Prime Minister David Cameron missed the vote while visiting flood-stricken areas in the south-west. Cameron's official spokesman declined to say which way the Prime Minister would have voted had he been able to attend Parliament. But he told a regular Westminster media briefing: 'While he understands the concerns that some have expressed, his view is that the time for this kind of approach has come.'

Health Secretary Jeremy Hunt was in favour of the move while Justice Secretary Chris Grayling was in the 'no' camp of those who said it is unenforceable. Deputy Prime Minister Nick Clegg has spoken out against attempts to 'sub-contract responsible parenting to the state' and pro-smoking groups have branded it an 'unnecessary intrusion'.

Shadow public health minister Luciana Berger welcomed the result but warned ministers not to 'kick this into the long grass'. She said: 'This is a great victory for child health which will benefit hundreds of thousands of young people across our country. It is a matter of child protection, not adult choice. The will of Parliament has been clearly expressed today and this must be respected. Ministers now have a duty to bring forward regulations so that we can make this measure a reality and put protections for children in place as soon as possible.

'A time-limited consultation may be necessary on the practical details of implementation, but we will be watching closely to ensure the Government don't try and kick this into the long grass.' AA president Edmund King said: 'MPs have said, no buts about it, endangering a child's health by smoking in the same car is unacceptable. The dangers from smoking in cars have long been recognised, such as distraction, littering and causing fires.

'These have been dealt with under existing laws but enforcement has proved difficult except after an incident. However, cases of people caught by speeding and other enforcement cameras while reading at the wheel, making V signs and other bad driving, mean that it is quite possible that smoking at the wheel with a child on board may be spotted. As has been the case with enforcing the ban on hand-held phones while driving, campaigns and legislation have been shown to reduce illegal behaviour afterwards. If a new law manages to make more adults think twice before lighting up with the kids on board, it will have helped.'

But Simon Clark, director of the smokers' group Forest, said he was 'disappointed but not surprised' by the decision. He added: 'The Government has been spineless in its response to Labour's initiative. Legislation will have very little impact because so few adults still smoke in cars carrying children. Those that do will carry on because it will be very difficult to enforce.

'The overwhelming majority of adult smokers know how to behave towards children and the law should reflect that. It shouldn't be used to stigmatise them as potentially unfit parents who can't be trusted to do the right thing without state intervention. If you believed everything you heard in the House about the threat to children's health it's a miracle anyone who was a child in the fifties and sixties, when a large majority of adults smoked, is still alive.

'Government has banned smoking in public places. Now they're going to ban it in a private place. The home will be next.'

Deborah Arnott, chief executive of health charity Ash (Action on Smoking and Health) said: "This is an historic victory for Parliament and for children's health. With support from across all political parties legislation has passed now both through the House of Lords and the Commons which will ensure cigarettes can be put in plain standardised packaging and smoking in cars with children under 18 can be made illegal.'

Professor John Britton of the Royal College of Physicians tobacco advisory group, added: 'Second-hand smoke has been strongly linked to a whole host of adverse health effects amongst children, including chest infections, asthma, ear problems and sudden infant death syndrome.

'Exposure to second-hand smoke in cars is particularly dangerous as it is a confined space leading to a high concentration of smoke. The introduction of a ban on smoking in cars with children will be a big step forward in protecting our children from the harm caused by passive smoking.'

The British Medical Association (BMA) has campaigned for a ban since 2011. Professor Sheila Hollins, chairwoman of the BMA's Board of Science, said: 'The outcome of this resounding vote is an important step forward in reducing tobacco harm by stopping children from being exposed to second-hand smoke in private vehicles.

'Children are still developing physically and, as a result, they are more susceptible to the harmful effects of second-hand smoke. Adults who smoke in the presence of children are not acting in the children's best interest; therefore it is the Government's duty to change legislation in order to protect them.'

10 February 2014

⇨ The above information is reprinted with kind permission from *Huffington Post UK*. Please visit www.huffingtonpost.co.uk for further information.

The last bastion: smoking to be banned in prisons

By Ian Dunt

The last bastion of free smoking in the UK is set to be shut down, after the Prison Service confirmed it was considering plans to ban smoking in prisons.

Prisons in south-west England are set to be part of a pilot ban, with the entirety of the prison system expected to follow suit by 2015.

About 80% of prisoners smoke and tobacco often functions as a form of currency on prison wings, leading many prison experts to warn that the move could trigger disorder.

'Prisons are going through unprecedented budget cuts, prison resources, staff resources have been cut,' Andrew Neilson of the Howard League for Penal Reform said.

'There may well be good intentions behind this policy proposal, but it will undoubtedly put a lot of pressure on jails which are already pretty stretched.'

Sadiq Khan, Labour's shadow justice secretary, said: 'Recent prison inspection reports show they are increasingly stretched on a daily basis battling simply to stop disturbances.

'A smoking ban in prisons without planning and resources seems an odd priority at a time when David Cameron's out of touch government has failed to deliver a so called "rehabilitation revolution".'

Under existing arrangements prisoners cannot smoke in indoor public areas but they are allowed to smoke in their cell as they are defined as 'domestic premises'.

Non-smoking prisoners are never forced to share a cell with a smoker.

The new plans would ban smoking in cells and even outdoor public areas like exercise yards.

'We are considering banning smoking across the prison estate and as part of this are looking at possible sites as early adopters,' a Prison Service spokesperson confirmed.

In a letter to senior staff and seen by *The Times*, the service said: 'You will no doubt be aware that the decision has been made that the time is right for the prison estate to adopt a tobacco and smoke-free policy to provide a smoke-free workplace/environment for our staff and prisoners.'

The ban is a key demand of the Prison Officers' Association since the ban on smoking in public places in 2007, with the union saying its members could otherwise be at risk of second-hand smoke.

20 September 2013

⇨ The above information is reprinted with kind permission from Politics.co.uk. Please visit www.politics.co.uk for further information.

New York bans tobacco sales to under-21s

Tobacco sales will be banned to under-21s in New York in a new health drive by mayor Michael Bloomberg.

The law will make it the first large US city or state to prohibit sales to young adults.

City health officials hope that raising the legal purchase age from 18 to 21 will lead to a big decline in smoking rates in a critical age group. Most smokers get addicted to cigarettes before 21, and then have trouble quitting.

The ban has limitations, in terms of its ability to stop young people from picking up the deadly habit. Teenagers can still possess tobacco legally. Children will still be able to steal cigarettes from their parents, take them from friends or buy them from the black-market dealers who are common in many neighbourhoods.

But City Health Commissioner Thomas Farley said the idea was to make it more inconvenient for young people to get started, especially teenagers who had previously had easy access to cigarettes through slightly older peers.

'Right now, an 18-year-old can buy for a 16-year-old,' he said. Once the law takes effect, in 180 days, he said, that 16-year-old would 'have to find someone in college or out in the workforce'.

Tobacco companies and some retailers had opposed the age increase, saying it would simply drive teenagers to the city's thriving black market.

'What are you really accomplishing? It's not like they are going to quit smoking. Why? Because there are so many other places they can buy cigarettes,' said Jim Calvin, president of the New York Association of Convenience Stores. 'Every 18-year-old who walks out of a convenience store is just going to go to the guy in the white van on the corner.'

Mr Bloomberg also introduced changes that will seek to keep the price of tobacco high by prohibiting coupons and other discounts and setting a minimum cigarette price of $10.50 (£6.52) per pack.

Large cigarette companies now commonly offer merchants incentives to run price promotions to bring in new customers.

'For someone who might be trying to quit smoking, it makes it easy for them to buy on impulse,' said Mr Farley.

Mr Calvin said the elimination of discounts would just further feed the drift away from legal cigarettes, and toward illicit supplies brought into the city by dealers who buy them at greatly reduced prices in other states, where tobacco taxes are low.

Both bills were passed by the City Council late last month. The legislation also prohibits the sale of small cigars in packages of less than 20 and increases penalties for retailers that violate sales regulations.

19 November 2013

⇨ The above information is reprinted with kind permission from *The Independent*. Please visit www.independent.co.uk for further information.

© *independent.co.uk*

European smoking bans: evolution of the legislation

More and more countries in Europe are adopting stricter legislation on smoking in public places. This information has been gathered by EPHA members, such as the European Network for Smoking Prevention (ENSP) and the European Respiratory Society on the progress of European countries in implementing anti-smoking legislation.

Introduction

In March 2004, Ireland became the first country in the world to impose an outright ban on smoking in workplaces. Irish legislation makes it an offence to smoke in workplaces, which has the effect of banning smoking in pubs and restaurants.

Following this successful example, Norway and Italy were next to follow suit. Other countries, such as Britain, Portugal and Sweden, have drafted plans to establish similar laws.

Croatia

In 2008, the Croatian Parliament passed a law making hospitals (except psychiatric services), schools (including universities), and nurseries smoke-free. In 2009, this law has been enforced, expanding the scope of the text to all enclosed public places including bars, restaurants and cafes.

From 2009 to 2010, the ban has been partially repealed. Establishments that are up to 50 square meters respecting very strict conditions can choose to allow tobacco consumption.

Cyprus

The protection of Health (smoking) Unified Laws 2002–2004 prohibit smoking in all public places, including places of entertainment (restaurants, bars, etc.) in all government buildings, public transport and in private cars carrying any passenger under 16. Separate smoking areas that are well ventilated will be introduced at the discretion of individual bar, cafe or restaurant owners.

Czech Republic

In April 2007, the Parliament passed an anti-smoking bill ought to limit smoking in restaurants and other public areas. Separate premises in restaurants, cafes and bars will have to be reserved for smokers.

England

On 1 July 2007, workplaces and enclosed public places in England became smoke-free environments. The Health Act 2006 defines enclosed public places and workplaces as being offices, factories, shops, pubs, bars, restaurants, membership clubs, public transport and work vehicles that are used by more than one person.

Greece

Since September 2010, Greece has implemented a new smoke-free regulation prohibiting the Greek population to smoke in bars, restaurants, cafes, workplaces (with no separated smoking room allowed) and public transport.

With more than 40% of its population smoking, Greece is the EU country with the highest rate of tobacco consumption.

Ireland

Ireland went completely smoke-free in 2004, including bars and restaurants.

Italy

Italian legislation has prohibited smoking in the workplace since 2005, including bars and restaurants. However, enclosed and separately ventilated rooms are permitted.

Latvia

Smoking is prohibited in many indoor public places and municipalities have the power to prohibit smoking in outdoor public places. However, smoking is permitted in bars and restaurants and other public catering establishments, however owners must set up no-smoking rooms.

Luxembourg

Anti-smoking legislation was recently passed by the Luxembourg Parliament. There will be a total ban on advertising and sponsoring, plus a ban on smoking in public places such as restaurants (although separate smoking rooms are permitted if these account for less than 25% of the total area of the venue) and cafés (with a ban in place during dining hours), total ban in schools as well as public buildings, buses and trains. Workplace regulations are more complex: the employer has the obligation to take all reasonable efforts to ensure that workers are protected from passive smoking.

The smoke-free legislation has been a real success in Luxembourg which is why the Government wants to further act in the protection of young people (in particular) from second-hand smoke.

Portugal

Portugal's smoking ban does not include bars and restaurants. Smoking is banned in healthcare, education and government facilities, as well as indoor workplaces, offices, theatres and cinemas with designated smoking areas. Smoking is banned on journeys that take less than an hour by public transport.

The Government is currently reviewing its smoke free legislation in the direction of smoke-free restaurants, nightclubs and bars. EPHA will keep you updated about the latest developments.

Scotland

Scotland implemented its smoking ban in March 2006. The ban covers all pubs, restaurants, bars, shops, cinemas, offices, hospitals, work vehicles and sports centres. Exemptions include private residential homes, private vehicles and designated rooms in care homes, prisons and hotels.

Spain

On 2 January 2011, Spain introduced one of the toughest pieces of smoke-free legislations in the EU. From now on, smoking is banned in bars, restaurants, discotheques, casinos, airports as well as in outside places such as outside hospitals and children's playgrounds. Only hotels are allowed to have 30% of their rooms open to smokers.

Sweden

In Sweden most workplaces are smoke-free. All bars, restaurants and nightclubs are also smoke-free. The law does allow for separately ventilated smoking rooms but less than 2% of Swedish facilities have chosen this option.

Wales

The Welsh Government first voted in favour of a smoking ban in 2003 and the ban on smoking in enclosed public places was introduced on 2 April 2007, three months ahead of the ban in England. Smoking is now banned in most public places, including restaurants, pubs and bars.

1 June 2012

⇨ The above information is reprinted with kind permission from epha. Please visit www.epha.org for further information.

© epha 2014

Fewer premature births due to smoking ban

New research has offered further evidence that a public smoking ban is helping cut the rate of premature births.

Findings reported in the *British Medical Journal* from a study of 600,000 births found three successive drops in babies born before 37 weeks.

Each occurred after a public smoking ban was introduced but there was no such trend in the period before the bans were put in place.

The latest study was conducted by a team at Hasselt University in Belgium and adds to similar findings from 2012 research in Scotland, though in that work researchers could not fully state the smoking ban was the cause of the change because pre-term births had started to drop before the ban.

However, the Belgian study looked at the rate of premature births after each phase of a smoking ban came into force in that country with a ban in public places and workplaces in 2006, restaurants the following year and bars serving food in 2010.

After each new phase, the rate of premature births fell and overall amounted to a fall of six premature babies in every 1,000 births.

Study leader Dr Tim Nawrot from Hasselt University said: 'Because the ban happened at three different moments, we could show there was a consistent pattern of reduction in the risk of preterm delivery.

'It supports the notion that smoking bans have public health benefits even from early life.'

The Royal College of Obstetricians and Gynaecologists welcomed the evidence that smoking bans have had a beneficial impact on pregnant women and their babies.

15 February 2013

⇨ The above information is reprinted with kind permission from Healthcare Today. Please visit www.healthcare-today.co.uk for further information.

© Mayden Foundation 2014

'Tobacco marketing harmful to kids'

84% of UK adults say children shouldn't be exposed to tobacco marketing; 79% agree it is harmful.

The majority of UK adults believe that children should not be exposed to any tobacco marketing, while four out of five of the 4,099 people interviewed believe that tobacco marketing is harmful to children, according to new data published by Cancer Research UK this week.

⇨ 84% of UK adults say that children shouldn't be exposed to tobacco marketing

⇨ 79% believe that tobacco marketing is harmful to children

⇨ 69% agree that the stylish, colourful branding, striking logos and distinctive packet design makes cigarettes more appealing to children

The results come in light of government consultations over whether to put all tobacco in packs of uniform size, shape and design, with large health warnings front and back.

⇨ When asked about how brand aware children are, 24% of parents and grandparents of children under the age of 18 said that they thought it was important for their oldest child or grandchild to have specific branded goods*

⇨ Although 51% said their oldest child or grandchild didn't ask for any branded goods, 84% of those that did, said that the child or grandchild in question was under 15 at the time

Brightly coloured

Cancer Research UK has recently released a film highlighting the response that brands and tobacco packaging elicits from children, while the charity also says that children respond positively to brightly coloured and slickly designed cigarette packs, with boys and girls finding different brands and packs appealing.

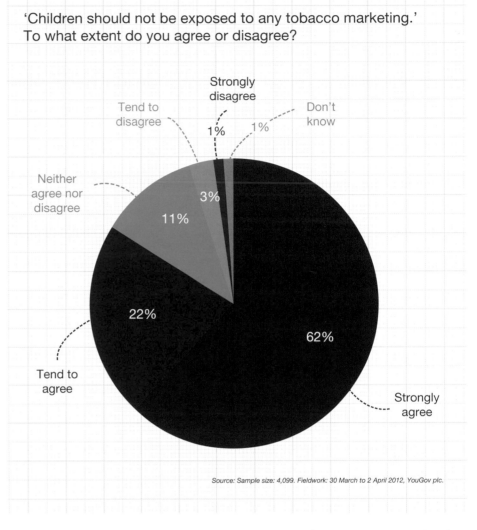

'Children should not be exposed to any tobacco marketing.' To what extent do you agree or disagree?

Strongly disagree 1%
Tend to disagree 1%
Don't know
Neither agree nor disagree 11%
3%
Tend to agree 22%
Strongly agree 62%

Source: Sample size: 4,099. Fieldwork: 30 March to 2 April 2012, YouGov plc.

Harpal Kumar, Cancer Research UK's chief executive, commented on the research, saying that 'the British people clearly support action to get rid of one of the last ways the tobacco industry can market its products. Most parents know their children are very attracted to certain brands and cleverly designed packaging plays a significant role in maintaining that attraction.'

'But when we are talking about tobacco then it's time to change the law. And our survey shows the vast majority of people support our stance on this.'

See more on Cancer Research UK's petition and campaign to remove branding from tobacco packaging www.theanswerisplain.org

** If the respondents had more than 1 child/grandchild under the age of 18, they were asked to think about the eldest child/grandchild who is under 18.

16 May 2012

⇨ The above information is reprinted with kind permission from YouGov. Please visit www.yougov.co.uk for further information.

© 2000-2014 YouGov plc

Thumbs down for Tobacco Products Directive

Thousands of UK consumers want the EU to abandon proposals to ban menthol cigarettes, increase size of health warnings and outlaw smaller packs of roll your own tobacco.

Proposals to ban menthol cigarettes, increase the size of health warnings and prohibit smaller packs of roll your own tobacco have received a firm thumbs down from thousands of consumers throughout the United Kingdom.

Ahead of the European Parliament vote on revisions to the European Tobacco Products Directive (TPD), the smokers' group Forest has revealed that its No Thank EU campaign against the measures generated almost 45,000 letters to MPs and MEPs.

According to Forest, 44,675 letters were e-mailed to politicians in Westminster and Brussels; 6,769 to MPs and 37,906 to UK MEPs.

Simon Clark, director of Forest, said: 'The response to our campaign highlights how strongly people feel about these illiberal and potentially irresponsible measures.

'There is no evidence the Directive will reduce smoking rates among children and every chance it will encourage illicit trade. Meanwhile, law-abiding adults

will be prohibited from buying products they have purchased and enjoyed for many years.'

Forest campaigns manager Angela Harbutt added: 'The biggest issue we faced was lack of public awareness of the EU's plans. We estimate that three quarters of the ten million smokers in the UK are completely in the dark about the proposals.

'When consumers were told about them they were furious and only too happy to write to their elected representatives.'

8 October 2013

⇨ The above information is printed with kind permission from Forest. Please visit www.forestonline.org for further information.

© Forest 2014

Did you know?

Doctors have recently suggested that the UK Government introduces new legislation to stop anyone born after the year 2000 from buying cigarettes. They say that this would gradually introduce a complete ban on tobacco products, save millions of pounds a year in smoking-related healthcare costs and prevent the vulnerable teenage age-group from taking up smoking at a young age.

TMA responds to the Government's decision not to introduce plain packaging

The Tobacco Manufacturers' Association (TMA) welcomes the Government's decision not to introduce plain packaging of tobacco products. Despite claims that the majority of the public support plain packaging, the UK public consultation on standardised packaging of tobacco products drew the largest ever response to a public consultation, almost 500,000 people expressed their opposition to plain packaging – two-thirds more than the number in favour. This unprecedented response represented views from thousands of members of the public as well as retailers, packaging companies, marketing and design firms, manufacturers, wholesalers, politicians, employers, employees, business groups, trade unions, the Intellectual Property community, international business, trade associations and the law enforcement community.

Jaine Chisholm Caunt, Secretary General of the TMA, commented:

'Plain packaging would have been an assault on UK business in an already tough economic environment. Plain packs would be far easier to copy and would therefore be a gift to the criminal gangs behind the illegal trade in tobacco and increase the £8 million per day that is currently lost to the UK Treasury as a result of this crime.

'At best, plain packaging would have no impact on youth smoking as there is no credible evidence that packaging is a factor in underage smoking. At worst, it could have actually increased youth smoking by driving up the availability of smuggled tobacco being sold by criminals in local communities. These illegal traders do not care who they sell to and frequently target children. The percentage of children who smoke in the UK is at an historic low – around 5%. We feel the Government should reduce

this figure still further by tackling children's access to tobacco through greater investment in enforcement action and tougher penalties targeted at illegal tobacco gangs and by making proxy purchasing of tobacco illegal, as it is for alcohol.'

Notes

1. The TMA is the Trade Association for tobacco manufacturers in the UK. Its three members are British American Tobacco (BAT), Imperial Tobacco and Japan Tobacco International (JTI).

2. The UK tobacco industry employs over 5,700 people in the UK and generates £12.1 billion per year in excise and VAT. Collectively with its UK supply chain, it supports a further 66,000 UK jobs and generates £2.1 billion GVA.

3. The TMA and its member companies are committed to addressing youth access prevention by supporting retailers through the 'No ID, No Sale' and CitizenCard campaigns and working in partnership with enforcement agencies, including HMRC to tackle the illicit trade in tobacco.

12 July 2013

⇨ The above article is a Media Statement, made publicly available by the Tobacco Manufacturers' Association. Please visit www.the-tma.org.uk for further information.

Scotland aims to be smoke-free by 2034 but what about e-cigs?

An article from The Conversation.

By Lisa Rutherford, Research Director, ScotCen Social Research at ScotCen Social Research

Given just how well established anti-smoking campaigns in Britain now are, many of today's smokers, and younger smokers in particular, have taken up the habit with at least some awareness of the damaging consequences of smoking on their long-term health. And despite these campaigns, the number of people smoking is still too high – particularly in Scotland, where, according to the Scottish Health Survey, one in four adults continues to smoke every day compared with around one in five in England and Wales.

In comparison to some of the more complex messages that public health campaigns need to get across, such as how many minutes a week we should all be active or how many units of alcohol we should be drinking, the message about tobacco harm is simple. So there is clearly more work to be done and the reasons behind smoking uptake still need to be fully understood.

The big picture

Each year, tobacco use is associated with around a quarter of all deaths in Scotland. It accounts for 56,000 hospital admissions, and costs NHS Scotland £400 million in treating smoking-related illnesses. It's an issue that bears consequences not only on those who smoke, but for Scottish society and its economy.

Since the Scottish Health Survey began in 1995, smoking among adults has declined by nearly 10%. The number of cigarettes being smoked has fallen too, from an average of 15-a-day to just over 12. Almost a third (29%) of those who smoke every day are between 25 and 44, making them the largest proportion of smokers.

Vast inequalities exist though. Those living in the country's most deprived areas are more than three times as likely as those living in areas of least deprivation to smoke.

In March 2013, the Scottish government published *Creating a Tobacco-Free Generation*, an ambitious new tobacco control strategy that aims to create a smoke-free Scotland by 2034. The strategy puts Scotland right up there as a world leader on tobacco control. The standardisation of packaging of tobacco products, prohibition of tobacco vending machines, and a restriction on the display of all tobacco and smoking-related products as laid out in the strategy will also all serve to help undermine the marketing efforts of tobacco companies.

The first of the strategy's milestones is to reduce prevalence to 17% by 2016. We therefore have a few more years to wait before we get a sense of just how ambitious the aim for a smoke-free generation is. It should be taken as read that the tobacco industry are watching on with great interest.

E-cigarette bans

The increased profile and availability of e-cigarettes has thrown a bit of a spanner in the works. Are they a stepping stone to tobacco use or if properly regulated could they act as a useful alternative to cigarettes? The long-term effects of e-cigarettes are not yet known. They may in time prove to be a useful quitting aid but as yet there is little evidence to support this. In the meantime, sales of e-cigarettes have increased by 340% in the past year while in the same period sales of licensed nicotine replacement products has slowed.

The danger lies in e-cigarettes use, or 'vaping', becoming a way of simply replacing one habit, proven to be damaging to health, with an alternative habit, about which little is currently known. Until we know more about their long-term health effects then perhaps the focus should be on discouraging habitual nicotine use more generally. It's encouraging to see that Glasgow's Commonwealth Games is the latest event to have banned the use of e-cigarettes from its venues in the same way tobacco smoking has been banned. This follows on from initiatives by other organisations including ScotRail, Starbucks and Wetherspoons pubs, none of whom allow 'vaping'.

We've also changed the Scottish Health Survey in 2014 to include questions on e-cigarette use for the first time. This means we will soon have robust data on the prevalence of e-cigarette use in Scotland, how it varies across different groups in society and how it relates to other health behaviours.

A recent EU Directive will also clarify the status of the e-cigarette as a product. The framework allows products to 'opt in' to medicines regulation or, failing that, be subject to a range of new controls which include safety and quality requirements as well as restrictions around advertising. With legislation to ban the sale of e-cigarettes to under-18s already passed in England and Wales, it is likely that Scotland will follow soon.

There are currently also no specific guidelines governing e-cigarette advertising but the Committee of Advertising Practice recently launched a public consultation on the marketing of e-cigarettes after one prime-time advert attracted over 1,000 complaints. The consultation ends in April and any new rules arising out of the consultation are expected to be implemented soon after.

Good news

The good news is that, according to a recent survey by Ash Scotland, Smoking among young teenagers is at its lowest level since 1990, an indication, perhaps, that this generation has taken more notice of – or

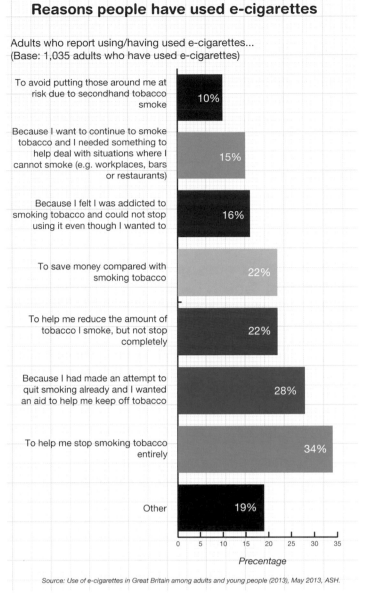

Reasons people have used e-cigarettes

Adults who report using/having used e-cigarettes...
(Base: 1,035 adults who have used e-cigarettes)

- To avoid putting those around me at risk due to secondhand tobacco smoke — 10%
- Because I want to continue to smoke tobacco and I needed something to help deal with situations where I cannot smoke (e.g. workplaces, bars or restaurants) — 15%
- Because I felt I was addicted to smoking tobacco and could not stop using it even though I wanted to — 16%
- To save money compared with smoking tobacco — 22%
- To help me reduce the amount of tobacco I smoke, but not stop completely — 22%
- Because I had made an attempt to quit smoking already and I wanted an aid to help me keep off tobacco — 28%
- To help me stop smoking tobacco entirely — 34%
- Other — 19%

Precentage

Source: Use of e-cigarettes in Great Britain among adults and young people (2013), May 2013, ASH.

been perhaps been more exposed to – effective anti-smoking campaigning.

We know from the latest Scottish Health Survey that 73% of smokers would like to stop and 41% have tried to quit on at least three occasions, so most smokers clearly want to change their behaviour. The challenge is to help and support these people give up, protecting others from second-hand exposure and fostering an environment where young people in Scotland do not want to take up smoking. In tandem with this is the challenge for the health community to figure out where e-cigarettes fit in with this in regards to nicotine addiction and harm reduction.

12 March 2014

⇨ The above information is reprinted with kind permission from The Conversation. Please visit www.theconversation.com for further information.

Indonesia's tobacco children

Indonesia is in the grip of a smoking epidemic with the proportion of child smokers rising dramatically. Jonathan Miller reports for Channel 4 News ahead of his investigation for Unreported World.

By Jonathan Miller, Foreign Affairs Correspondent

The health minister of Indonesia, the world's fastest-growing cigarette market, has pledged to sign a United Nations treaty developed in response to what the UN's World Health Organization has branded 'the globalisation of the tobacco epidemic'.

'Indonesia is among a tiny handful of countries, which include North Korea and Zimbabwe, not to have signed the UN tobacco control convention...'

Dr Nafsiah Mboi's intention to sign the agreement will put her at loggerheads with Indonesia's powerful tobacco industry, a backbone of the national economy which provides millions of jobs.

In advance of a meeting of the WHO Framework Convention on Tobacco Control, scheduled to be held in the South Korean capital, Seoul, next week, the minister said an alarming increase in the number of child smokers in Indonesia has galvanised her determination to see the treaty signed.

Indonesia is among a tiny handful of countries, which include North Korea and Zimbabwe, not to have signed

the UN tobacco control convention, which greatly restricts advertising, promotion and sponsorship of tobacco products and bans sales of cigarettes to minors.

Speaking to Channel 4's *Unreported World*, Dr Mboi said the power of the tobacco lobby in Indonesia had, in the past, made it politically difficult to sign up to the UN agreement.

'A lot of people in the government said 'we should not stop this because of the revenues. We've got the revenues from the tobacco tax, we are providing... employment for so many million people.'

'...one teenager in four is a regular smoker before they turn 16...

Asked whether her decision to take on the industry, given its importance to the Indonesian economy, would not make her unpopular, she replied: 'So what? People who started smoking between five and nine years of age... has increased seven-fold. It's a sin. Why are they protecting the tobacco industry when they know that so many young kids become the victims.'

'Last year [2011], tobacco companies spent £142 million advertising in Indonesia'

More than two-in-three Indonesian adult males smoke. There are estimated to be around 90 million smokers in a country of 238 million people. The proportion of children who regularly smoke is rising and one teenager in four is a regular smoker before they turn 16.

Respiratory specialists consider this to be a health time bomb.

The Channel 4 team filmed many children who were hooked on cigarettes up to four times the strength of the strongest legally on sale in Britain.

'My Life, My Adventure'

Many said they were drawn to the habit by ubiquitous advertising, particularly television advertisements – which

YOUR GOVERNMENT THANKS YOU...

TOBACCO INDUSTRY

INDONESIAN YOUTH

would be banned were Indonesia to sign up to the UN tobacco control protocol.

Of all the TV ads, the best known are those for Djarum Super. They are known as 'My Life, My Adventure', a big-budget production, which sets out to associate the brand with the magnificence of Indonesia's most rugged scenery. It features a health warning at the end: 12 frames (half a second) long.

Cigarette companies sponsor rock concerts, jazz festivals and sporting events – including football, badminton, cycling and adventure sports. Last year, tobacco companies spent £142 million advertising in Indonesia.

The Indonesian cabinet is reportedly split on the issue of whether to sign because the industry is a mainstay of the national economy. The taxation of tobacco companies contributes ten per cent of national revenue, making it as crucial to Indonesia as the financial sector is to Britain. It also provides around ten million jobs, directly and indirectly.

Nine out of ten Indonesian smokers smoke 'kreteks' – strong, clove-flavoured cigarettes, the aroma of which infuses the entire archipelago. In recent years, western cigarette giants Philip Morris (the makers of Marlboro) and British American Tobacco have bought into the Indonesian kretek market.

In 2005, Philip Morris International bought a controlling share of a leading Indonesian tobacco firm, Sampoerna, for US$5 billion. Four years later, BAT bought Indonesia's fourth largest cigarette company, Bentoel, for US$494 million.

A senior insider from the industry, who met the Channel 4 team in Jakarta, said the big foreign firms were now 'milking a cash cow'.

In September this year, the chief financial officer of Philip Morris International told an international conference that his firm's 'excellent results' in Asia - which were, he said, 'driven in particular by Indonesia' had 'more than offset a substantial decline in the EU region'.

A short distance from a village in which the Channel 4 team filmed a six-year-old smoker - who has recently cut back from smoking 20-a-day – children between 11 and 12 years of age were filmed picking and sorting tobacco which was supplied to Bentoel, the BAT subsidiary, and other companies.

'Child labour in the tobacco industry is dangerous work,' said Priyono Adi Nugroho, of Indonesia's Child Protection Institute. 'Children are not supposed to be working. Children are supposed to go to school, study and play. Instead, they work in an industry which produces cigarettes. Then they start smoking themselves and see it as nothing out of the ordinary.'

In a statement to Channel 4, BAT said it took a strong stance against child labour and always encouraged its representatives to tell farmers what its corporate policy was on child labour. BAT's Bentoel Group said it did not employ any child labour, either directly or indirectly and said it was 'actively involved in programmes to prevent the exploitative use of child labour in leaf-growing areas'.

Jonathan Miller's documentary *Indonesia's Tobacco Children was shown* on *Unreported World* on 9 November 2012 at 7.30pm.

9 November 2012

⇨ The above information is reprinted with kind permission from Channel 4 News. Please visit www.channel4.com/news for further information.

Summary of global youth tobacco surveys in Indonesia among 13- to 15-year-olds, 2004 to 2006						
Responses	**Beksai**	**Medan**	**C. Java**	**Sumatra**	**Surakarta**	**Jakarta**
Currently use tobacco (%)						
Male	34.8	40.5	25.0	24.0	29.3	32.1
Female	9.4	8.1	4.3	5.0	3.4	7.4
Among children that currently smoke, % that tried to stop in the past year	88.7	88.4	83.3	93.3	90.7	91.8
Among all children, % that:						
were exposed to second-hand smoke outside home	76.1	79.5	81.1	81.0	79.7	81.6
saw a cigarette billboard in the last 30 days	88.8	91.8	92.7	93.4	94.7	93.2
Source: Centres for Disease Control and Prevention, Global Youth Tobacco Surveys Country Fact Sheets.						

Key facts

- Every year, around 100,000 people die from smoking, with many more deaths caused by smoking-related illnesses. (page 1)

- Smoking increases your risk of developing more than 50 serious health conditions. (page 1)

- Breathing in second-hand smoke increases a non-smoker's risk of developing lung cancer or heart disease by about 25%. (page 1)

- Tobacco smoke (tar) contains over 4,000 chemicals and many have effects on various parts of the human body. (page 2)

- Smoking has been linked to the amputations of 2,000 limbs a year. (page 2)

- Every year, nearly three in ten smokers try to quit. (page 4)

- The highest recorded level of smoking among men in Great Britain was 82% in 1948, of which 65% smoked manufactured cigarettes. (page 6)

- There are about ten million adult cigarette smokers in Great Britain and about 15 million ex-smokers. (page 6)

- In 2012 38% of men and 24% of women smoked hand-rolled cigarettes. (page 6)

- In March 2011 the Coalition Government launched its Tobacco Control Plan for England in which it set out ambitions to reduce adult smoking prevalence to 18.5% or less by 2015. (page 6)

- In 2011, 63% of smokers said they would like to stop smoking altogether. (page 7)

- In 2011, 16% of all smokers had their first cigarette within five minutes of waking. (page 7)

- In 2011, among smokers of 20 or more cigarettes a day, 35% smoked their first cigarette of the day within five minutes of waking, compared to just 3% of those smoking fewer than ten a day. (page 7)

- About nine out of ten lung cancers are caused by smoking. (page 8)

- If you smoke 20 or more cigarettes a day, your risk of having a stroke can be up to six times higher than that of a non-smoker. (page 8)

- Smoking can prematurely age your skin between ten and 20 years, and you're more likely to have facial wrinkles at a younger age. (page 8)

- If you smoke five cigarettes a day for one year you will spend £644. (page 9)

- If you smoke 20 cigarettes a day for a year you will spend £2,577. (page 9)

- More than 200,000 under 16s start smoking in the UK every year. (page 12)

- Research recently found that 22% of people surveyed could not name any symptoms of lung cancer. (page 16)

- When you quit smoking, within the first six hours, the heart rate deceases and blood pressure drops. Within a week, taste and smell improve and lungs begin to clear. After ten years, the risk of lung cancer is lower than if the individual had continued smoking and by 15 years the risk of heart attack and stroke returns to those of someone who has never smoked. (page 17)

- 54% of doctors think the NHS should have the right to withhold non-emergency treatment to patients unless they lose weight or stop smoking. (page 22)

- 88% of smokers admit they regret taking it up in the first place because it is now showing in their appearance. (page 25)

- Ireland went completely smoke-free in 2004, including bars and restaurants. (page 31)

- 62% of people strongly agree that children should not be exposed to tobacco marketing. (page 33)

Ammonia

A chemical found in cleaning fluids, ammonia is inhaled during smoking.

Arsenic

A deadly poison used in insecticides, arsenic is contained in tobacco and is therefore inhaled during smoking.

Cadmium

A metal used in batteries, also contained in tobacco.

Cigarette

A paper tube filled with tobacco which is lit at one end and inhaled orally (smoked). There are many slang words for cigarettes, including fags, tabs, smokes and cigs/ciggies. Cigarettes can be bought pre-prepared or hand-rolled. Most modern cigarettes contain a spongy filter which reduces the amount of poisonous chemicals inhaled while smoking: however, a large part of these substances are still absorbed and smoking therefore poses a substantial health risk.

Tobacco can also be inhaled using cigars and pipes, or it can be chewed. There are health risks associated with all methods of using tobacco.

Carbon monoxide

A toxic gas released when something is burnt incompletely, found in tobacco smoke.

Cyanide

A poisonous compound, found in tobacco smoke.

e-cigarette

An electronic cigarette. Smoking an e-cigarette is known as 'vaping' (play on the word 'vapours' which emit from the device). There is debate as to how safe e-cigarettes are, as more research is needed on the effects of the vapours produced. Some people use e-cigarettes as a quitting aid to help them cut down or stop smoking completely. However, some people feel that the variety of flavours, such as blueberry or orange, and brightly coloured devices might be appealing to children and could be a gateway to smoking. There is also currently debate on whether e-cigarettes should be included in the smoking band and banned in public places, just like real cigarettes.

Formaldehyde

A chemical used to preserve corpses. Formaldehyde is contained in tobacco.

Nicotine

An addictive chemical compound found in the nightshade family of plants that makes up about 0.6–3.0% of dry weight of tobacco. It is the nicotine contained in tobacco which causes smokers to become addicted, and many will use Nicotine Replacement Therapy such as patches, gum or electronic cigarettes to help them deal with cravings while quitting.

Passive smoking/second-hand smoke

Passive smoking refers to the inhalation of tobacco smoke by someone other than the smoker: for example, a parent smoking near their children may expose them to the poisonous chemicals in the second-hand smoke from their cigarette. This has been shown to have a negative impact on the passive smoker's health.

The smoking ban

The Health Act 2006, which came into force in England and Wales on 1 July 2007, made it illegal to smoke in all enclosed public places and enclosed work places (similar bans were already in place in other parts of the UK). This has led to much debate about the balance between public health and individual freedoms.

Third-hand smoke

Once second-hand smoke has disappeared, tobacco smoke still lingers even after a cigarette has been put out – this is known as third-hand smoke. It clings to fabrics and people can be exposed to particles through inhalation, ingestion or skin contact. This can be particularly dangerous to young children because they are more likely to crawl on the floor and eat from their hands without washing them first, ingesting the toxins into their system.

Tar

A mixture of chemicals (including formaldehyde, arsenic and cyanide). About 70 per cent of the tar in a cigarette is left in smokers' lungs, causing a range of serious lung conditions.

Tobacco

Tobacco is a brown herb-like substance produced from the dried leaves of tobacco plants. The tobacco used in cigarettes contains many substances dangerous to the user when inhaled, including tar, which can cause lung cancer, and nicotine, which is highly addictive. Nevertheless, around 21 per cent of adults in the UK are smokers.

Assignments

Brainstorming

⇨ In small groups, brainstorm to find out what you know about smoking and health. Consider the following questions:

- are cigarettes bad for you?

- what are the long-term and short-term health effects of smoking?

- why do you think people start smoking?

- what are e-cigarettes?

- what are the laws surrounding smoking?

⇨ Create a mind map on a large piece of paper to demonstrate your ideas.

Research

⇨ Look at the timeline on page three and do some research to find out more about the history of smoking. Create your own timeline.

⇨ Do some research and find out about a famous person or celebrity who died from a smoking-related illness. Create a short presentation about this person and perform your presentation for the rest of your class.

⇨ Over the course of a week, take note of any films, adverts or television programs which show people smoking and whether it is portrayed in a positive or negative light. Share your findings with the rest of your class.

⇨ Research cigarette advertising from another decade, e.g. the 1950s and create a PowerPoint presentation exploring what this shows about attitudes towards smoking.

Oral

⇨ In pairs, role play a situation in which one of you is a smoker and the other is an ex-smoker trying to persuade your friend to quit. Take it in turns to play each role and think about what you could say to encourage your friend to see the benefits of quitting.

⇨ Why do people start smoking, even when they know it is bad for their health? Discuss in small groups and feedback to the rest of your class.

⇨ As a class, stage a debate in which half of you argue that smoking should be banned in prisons, and the other half argues that it should not.

⇨ Do you think that cigarettes being sold in plain packages will discourage people from smoking? Discuss in small groups.

⇨ What do you think to the suggestion that the UK Government should ban anyone born after the year 2000 from buying cigarettes? Discuss as a class.

Design

⇨ Create a plan for a website that will inform young people about the health risks of smoking. Decide how many pages your website will have and write some short descriptions of the information that will be on each page. Then think of a name for your site and draw some sketches to show what it will look like.

⇨ Design a poster that highlights the signs of lung cancer.

⇨ Design a poster that highlights the negative effects smoking can have on your appearance.

⇨ Imagine you have been asked to run a smoking awareness day at your school. What would the day include? In pairs, plan some activities, talks, etc. and then create some promotional material to raise awareness of your day.

⇨ Design a television advert that will raise awareness of the effects of passive smoking on pets and children.

Reading/Writing

⇨ What is tobacco? Write a summary of no more than one side of A4 exploring this question.

⇨ Write an essay exploring the positive and negative aspects of e-cigarettes.

⇨ Write a blog post exploring whether you agree or disagree that people who smoke should be denied treatment for non-life threatening illnesses, until they quit smoking.

⇨ Write a letter to your local MP arguing against a ban on smoking in cars with child passengers.

⇨ How can we encourage young people to stop smoking? Write a newspaper article exploring your ideas.

⇨ Read the article on page 36 *Scotland aims to be smoke-free by 2034 but what about e-cigs?* Write a summary for your school newspaper.

addiction 3, 4–5

additives and flavours prohibition, Tobacco Product Directive 27

advertising and child smoking, Indonesia 39

age
  and cigarette smoking 6
  for purchasing tobacco, New York 30

appearance, effects of smoking 8–9, 25

bans on smoking see smoking bans

betel quid 10

brain and mood, effect of nicotine 4, 5

branding of products, influence on children 33

Breath of Addiction (film) 15

cancer 1, 8

chemical content
  of cigarettes 3
  of e-cigarettes 11, 13

chewing tobacco 10

child labour, tobacco industry 9, 39

children
  and e-cigarette marketing 12
  and passive smoking 14, 28–9
  and smoking 6, 20, 38–9
  and tobacco marketing 33

chronic obstructive pulmonary disease (COPD) 8

cigarettes
  chemical content 3
  consumption trends 6–7
  packaging 27, 35

costs of smoking 9, 21, 26

Croatia, smoking ban 31

Cyprus, smoking ban 31

Czech Republic, smoking ban 31

deforestation and tobacco production 9

dependence on cigarette smoking 7

doctors, views on restricting treatment of smokers 22–3

e-cigarettes 11–12, 13, 25, 37
  reasons for use 11–12, 37
  safety 11, 13
  and Tobacco Product Directive 27

effects of smoking 2–3, 4, 5
  on appearance 8–9, 25
  on health 1, 2–3, 4, 8–9

England, smoking ban 31

environmental costs of smoking 9

European countries, smoking bans 31–2

fertility, effects of smoking 8

films
  depicting smoking, impact on young people 18–19
  on third-hand smoke 15

giving up see stopping smoking

Greece, smoking ban 31

gutkha 10

health risks of smoking 1, 2–3, 4, 8–9, 10
  passive smoking 14

health treatment restriction on smokers and obese people 22–3

health warnings on packaging 27

heart and blood circulation effects of smoking 1, 4, 8

history of smoking 3

hookah smoke (shisha) 2, 3, 10

impurities in cigarettes 3

Indonesia, child smokers 38–9

Ireland, smoking ban 31

Italy, smoking ban 31

labelling and Tobacco Product Directive 27

Latvia, smoking ban 31

law on cigarette sales 3

legal purchase age for tobacco, New York 30

lifestyle rationing of healthcare 22–3

lung cancer symptoms awareness 16

lung damage 1, 8

Luxembourg, smoking ban 31

marketing, influence on children
  e-cigarettes 12
  tobacco 33, 39

monetary costs of smoking 9, 21, 26

New York, raising tobacco purchase age 30

NHS Stop Smoking service 10, 24

nicotine 3, 4, 5

obesity and restriction of health treatment 22–3

paan 10

packaging
  plain 35
  and Tobacco Product Directive 27

passive smoking see secondhand smoke

pets and passive smoking 14

plain packaging 35

pollution, environmental 9

Portugal, smoking ban 31

pregnancy, risks of smoking 1

premature births reduced following smoking ban 32

prisons, ban on smoking 29

purchase age for tobacco, New York 30

reasons for smoking 4–5
  e-cigarettes 11–12

relaxation effect of nicotine 5

Roy, Satyajit 15

safety, e-cigarettes 11, 13
Scotland 36–7
  smoking ban 32
secondhand smoke 1, 14
  in cars 28–9
sex, effects of smoking 8
shisha 2, 3, 10
slim cigarettes ban, Tobacco Product Directive 27
smokefree movie policies 19
smokers
  age 6
  consumption habits 7
  restriction of health treatment 22–3
smoking bans 31–2
  in cars with child passengers 28–9
  and premature births reduction 32
  in prisons 29
smoking
  effects see effects of smoking
  history of 3
  reasons for 4–5
  Scotland 36–7
  trends 6–7
social smoking 17
socialisation and smoking 5
socio-economic group and cigarette smoking 6–7
Spain, smoking ban 32
stimulant effect of nicotine 5
Stop Smoking service (NHS) 10, 24
stopping smoking 5, 10, 17, 21, 26
  health benefits 9, 17, 21
Stoptober challenge 26

surgery
  restrictions for smokers and obese people 22–3
  risks to smokers 9
Sweden, smoking ban 32

third-hand smoke 15
tobacco 2–3
tobacco industry
  child labour 9, 39
  and e-cigarettes 12
  environmental costs 9
  and worker health 9
Tobacco Product Directive 27, 34
tobacco products
  in films 18–19
  gateway effects of e-cigarettes 12, 13
  marketing, impact on children 33, 39
  purchase age, New York 30
  see also cigarettes

vaping see e-cigarettes

Wales, smoking ban 32
water pipes (shisha) 2, 3, 10

young people, influence of smoking in films 18–19

Acknowledgements

The publisher is grateful for permission to reproduce the material in this book. While every care has been taken to trace and acknowledge copyright, the publisher tenders its apology for any accidental infringement or where copyright has proved untraceable. The publisher would be pleased to come to a suitable arrangement in any such case with the rightful owner.

Images

Cover, page iii and pages 18 and 19: iStock, page 10 © Sean Sharifi, page 15: iStock, page 17: MorgueFile, page 24: iStock, page 25 © David Goehring, page 30 © Jonas Nilsson Lee, page 32: iStock, page 34 © A J Garrison, page 35 © Alvimann, page 36 © iStock.

Illustrations

Don Hatcher: pages 2 and 22. Angelo Madrid: pages 5 and 32. Simon Kneebone: pages 20 and 38.

Additional acknowledgements

Editorial on behalf of Independence Educational Publishers by Cara Acred.

With thanks to the Independence team: Mary Chapman, Sandra Dennis, Christina Hughes, Jackie Staines and Jan Sunderland.

Cara Acred

Cambridge

May 2014